Galatians
Gospel of Freedom

David Allan Hubbard

Galatians
Gospel of Freedom

Word Books, Publisher
Waco, Texas

First Printing, June 1977
Second Printing, March 1979

ISBN 0-8499-2800-1
Library of Congress catalog card number: 77-075451
Printed in the United States of America

CONTENTS

INTRODUCTION

Galatians is a passionate letter, even angry at times. Some of the customary niceties of letter writing Paul omitted here. In the introduction, he paused not at all to thank his hearers or their God for any spiritual grace or virtue. His tongue was racing to get to the center of the problems. No more than a surgeon in the emergency ward would stop to chit-chat with a hemorrhaging patient did Paul waste time either on compliments or casual comments.

His first words, after the introduction, were, "I am astonished that you are so quickly deserting him who called you in the grace of Christ and turning to a different gospel . . ." (Gal. 1:6). This tone of astonishment set the mood for the entire gospel. From beginning to end Paul was chagrined, baffled, puzzled, dismayed, amazed at the fickleness of the Galatians, as they toyed with the possibility of substituting religious regulations for the freedom of a gospel that promised salvation by grace to all who believe in Christ Jesus.

So strong was Paul's amazement that he once addressed his friends with these words, "O foolish Galatians! Who has bewitched you, before whose eyes Jesus Christ was publicly portrayed as crucified?" (Gal. 3:1). At the heart of Paul's astonishment stood a cross. There, in the death of his Son, God had wrought history's great surprise. He had made forgiveness of sins and full salvation possible apart from human laws and religious practices. A gift had been offered by the outstretched hands of God himself, and that gift was now being kicked aside and trampled by foolish and ungrateful men and women. The door to fellowship opened wide by Jesus' death was now being barred by the turnstile of circumcision. Misguided teachers were requiring Gentiles in Galatia to become Jews before they could truly be Christians.

That was a moment for passion, not calmness. And every fiber in the Apostle Paul responded to make clear the issues of freedom. The way to the cross is the road to freedom—from sin, from guilt, from legal regulations, from religious superstitions, from fear of demon power. All paths away from that cross lead to slavery—slavery in a hundred different forms. Nothing less than life and death was at stake in the Galatians' decision.

Just who the Galatians were has been a matter of great discussion. Galatia may refer to an ethnic area in central Asia Minor where Galatian tribes lived. Or it may be used of a political area, the Roman province of Galatia, that included part of the central region and also extended farther south, taking in the familiar towns of Lystra, Iconium, and Derbe, which Paul had visited (Acts 14). Since there is no specific record of a journey to the more northern tribal area of Galatia, it is more likely that it was the Christians in the southern part of the province whom Paul addressed.

The date of the letter has been a matter of some dispute. Suggestions range from about A.D. 48, which would make it Paul's earliest New Testament writing, to about A.D. 56, where it would be grouped with

2 Corinthians and Romans, letters closely akin to Galatians in spirit and content. The tendency in recent scholarship has been to lean toward the earlier date. Happily our understanding of its teaching is little affected by the questions of exact place and date.

There is no question as to who wrote the letter. It has the fingerprints of Paul's doctrine, spirit, and language all over it. And there is no doubt about its purpose: it is a stalwart defense of Christian truth against the error of legalism; it is a ringing gospel of Christian freedom to churches in danger of substituting human effort for divine grace.

This little study is not at all a verse by verse commentary. Its aim is to sketch the main themes of the book against the backdrop of the problems of the early Church and then to give them application to our spiritual problems today.

In various forms these lessons were shared with groups whose questions and comments improved their quality measurably. The Young Presbyterian Ministers' Fellowship showed patience and long suffering at a conference at Mt. Hermon, California, in April, 1974. The Christian Endeavor of Australia was a thoughtful audience at its biennial convention in Sydney during January, 1974. My thanks go to both of these groups, as they do to the listeners of "The Joyful Sound" radio broadcast where these chapters were first heard in their present form. My wife Ruth gave her usual loving and careful attention to the editing. She was assisted in the typing by Janet Johns.

Freedom is not an ancient question alone. In the late twentieth century we still find it easier to be super-

stitious than to be trusting, to be anxious about the oc-
cult than to be confident in God, to wallow in our
failure than to rest in divine forgiveness, to fight for our
own righteousness than to let Christ be righteous for us.

Freedom is good news today because it still catches
us by surprise. It shows up all substitutes as sham. With
tight jaws and clenched fists our generation has boasted
of its freedom. It can hardly spell the word let alone
savor the experience.

Where do misguided rebels go to tell the difference
between their hostility and true freedom? Let them go
to Galatians and hear the good news that God has set
us free for love. Where do uptight conformists look
for release from anxieties about their failures or de-
liverance from pride in their successes? Let them look to
Galatians and read the good news that Christ has ac-
complished for us what we could never do for ourselves.

The early Church was rescued from strife, fear,
despair, and arrogance by the Galatian letter. The Ref-
ormation launched its sweeping changes to the notes
sounded by Paul in Galatians. At those two pivotal
points in Christian history, Galatians brought good
news when so many reports of human life seemed bad.

What it has done before, Galatians is prepared to do
again. The Holy Spirit is still astonished at our religious
foolishness. But he is still able to set us straight with the
word of forgiveness and new life. Galatians brings that
word as cogently and clearly as any part of Scripture.
It is the gospel of freedom because powerfully and pas-
sionately it confronts us with the freedom of the gospel.

I

Who Is Jesus Christ?

Galatians 1:1-5

Paul an apostle—not from men nor through man, but through Jesus Christ and God the Father, who raised him from the dead—and all the brethren who are with me,

To the churches of Galatia:

Grace to you and peace from God the Father and our Lord Jesus Christ, who gave himself for our sins to deliver us from the present evil age, according to the will of our God and Father; to whom be the glory for ever and ever. Amen.

She was about three years old at the time—our daughter, Mary. Her bright eyes flashed up at me as I finished the bedtime prayer. "I know who Jesus is," she beamed with great self-assurance. And my self-assurance matched hers, as I prepared myself for her answer. After all, not every three-year-old child has the benefit of growing up in the home of a Bible teacher and theologian, I boasted to myself.

"Tell daddy who Jesus is," I urged expectantly. Her

11

answer was not what I had hoped for. "He is the man with the mustache," Mary declared, peering up at the picture on the wall. I covered my disappointment with a quiet laugh. "That's right; he is." But I made some mental notes about the need for a more weighty theological curriculum in the Hubbard household.

Popular answers to the question, "Who is Jesus Christ?" have often been little more profound than Mary's comment was. The label *superstar* is a case in point. The name conjures up visions of a tennis champion charging the net at Wimbledon, of a powerful hitter watching his fiftieth home run of the season sail into the stands, of a movie actor feigning humility as he clutches the Oscar, of an opera tenor pushing through the curtain to repeated rounds of applause, of a rock singer proudly displaying her gold record.

The very title is misleading. *Superstar* smacks of competition among a group of peers, of achievement based on popular acclaim, of wealth and gaudy lifestyle. Few terms could be used less appropriately of Jesus.

Jesus is not a superstar; nor is he a folk hero of the counterculture. At first glance he may seem to be, as he exposes the hypocrisy of the Pharisees and purges the temple of its moneychangers. But these strong words and deeds were not fits of rage against the establishments of the day. They were aspects of a renewal that called every level of society—whether establishment or antiestablishment—to repentance. However much our restless young people may admire Jesus' kindness and marvel at his courage, they will balk like everyone else at his call to repentance. Once they really hear that call, they may revoke his hero's license.

"The man with the mustache" our daughter called

him—a reminder that people have struggled through the centuries to know who Jesus is. In the early years of the Church, one popular answer was that Jesus was a "wonder-worker." Stories grew that pictured the boy Jesus making clay pigeons and then slapping his hands while the pigeons snapped into life and took to flight.

Who is Jesus Christ? Another popular answer of those early years was "mystic teacher," a revealer of secret knowledge. In Egypt particularly, a whole encyclopedia of his teaching was developed. Only those who were initiated into the inner circle of believers could be privy to this superior knowledge.

Who is Jesus Christ? Even when he was here on earth, men and women found no simple answer to that question. "Now when Jesus came into the district of Caesarea Philippi, he asked his disciples, 'Who do men say that the Son of man is?' And they said, 'Some say John the Baptist, others say Elijah, and others Jeremiah or one of the prophets' " (Matt. 16:13–14).

Who is Jesus Christ? The popular answers have always had difficulty coping with his uniqueness. They focus on one feature of his ministry, or put him in a category with others whose pattern he appears to have followed: superstar, hero, miracle-worker, enlightened teacher, prophet.

Popular answers always have fallen short. That is why we need *official answers*. Jesus himself saw to it that we got them. He did that by appointing apostles —messengers specially chosen and officially commissioned to carry the good news. Not just any good news, but *the* good news of who Jesus is and what he has done.

It was this question of official status more than anything else that threatened to hinder the ministry of the Apostle Paul. We run head-on into this problem in the letter to the Galatians. A group of religious teachers had given their own popular answer to our key question. They viewed Jesus as a Jewish teacher who had come to make it possible for Gentiles to become Jews. If Gentiles practiced circumcision, observed the holy days, and kept the laws of diet and dress, then they were qualified to join God's family.

Paul opposed this teaching with the sternest kind of opposition. When he did, the teachers who were disturbing the Galatian Christians began a personal assault on his reputation: "Paul? What kind of apostle is he? Was he one of the original twelve? Did he live and travel with Jesus? Where did he get his knowledge of the gospel? What makes you think his interpretation is more reliable than ours?"

Fearful lest the newly born Christians be badly bruised by the batterings of questions like these, Paul seized quill and parchment and began to use them as sword and shield against his opponents. With incredible boldness he linked together the two dominant themes of his letter in the first few verses: his divine commission as an apostle, and the unique work of Jesus as Savior.

For us, as for Paul, these themes belong together. We have no valid information about who Jesus Christ is apart from the apostles. We know him through them, or we do not know him at all.

For the answer to any question, we are foolish if we do not go to the best possible source. Would we look for phone numbers in a cookbook? Would we try to find the football scores in a dictionary? If we are really serious about the question of who Jesus Christ is, we will go to the proper source—the writings of the apostles whom Jesus charged with the task of making him known.

At Jesus' insistence, Paul joined this group. That dramatic scene on the Damascus road was not just a conversion; it was a *commissioning*. Paul might have been converted by the preaching of the gospel and the prompting of the Spirit, as the rest of Christ's people have through the ages. But he could not have been commissioned as an apostle without a direct word from Jesus Christ and a personal meeting with him. That happened when Jesus intercepted him on the way to Damascus and changed his life. Paul knew who Jesus was firsthand, and he challenged his opponents to present credentials as substantial as his. "Paul an apostle," he began his letter, "—not from men nor through man, but through Jesus Christ and God the Father, who raised him from the dead . . ." (Gal. 1:1). His authority was not derived from a group of human leaders, nor was it a mere man that had appointed him. It was the risen Christ who sent him on this assignment. The *risen* Christ had appeared to him as to the others at an earlier time and ordered him to be a witness to the resurrection. And behind the words of Jesus was the full authority of God the Father.

Who is Jesus? Paul's response, then, was not another one of the popular answers. It had the official seal of Jesus himself on it. That means it must be read with care.

The One Who Bears the Names of God

Paul's conversion and commission produced some

startling changes in his thinking, perhaps none more startling than his eagerness to associate Jesus Christ with God. Blasphemy, he would have called this in his pre-Christian days. In fact, his heavy-handed persecution of Christians was based on his outrage at their view of Jesus. Now he shared that view. He accepted the Christian answer to the question, "Who is Jesus Christ?"

To Paul and his fellow believers, Jesus is the one who bears the names of God. "Paul an apostle—not from men nor through man, but through Jesus Christ and God the Father . . ." (Gal. 1:1). A Jew could scarcely have believed his ears at these words. Paul was linking the name of Jesus to the name of God the Father. More than that, Paul dared to put Jesus' name first.

The implication was obvious: Jesus was equal to the Father in power and glory. In other words, Jesus Christ was *God*. Lest there be any doubt, Paul went on to say: "Grace to you and peace from God the Father and our Lord Jesus Christ" (Gal. 1:3). Once again the close coordination, the firm link, between Jesus and God the Father was announced without apology.

The very titles of Jesus help to tell us who he is. Paul called him "Lord." When he did, he used the term *Kurios* that the Greek translation of the Old Testament had used for the divine name *Yahweh*, or *Jehovah*. Again we see the boldness of the early Christians: they gave to Jesus the loftiest, most sacred name given to God in the Old Testament. Jesus is the one who bears the names of God.

The title *Lord* also meant that Jesus was worthy of worship. The commandment said, "You shall have no other gods before me" (Exod. 20:3). Yet the first Christians confessed their faith this way: "Jesus is

Lord." The ruler of all life, the governor of history, the Lord to be adored and obeyed—these were the ideas implicit in that creed. And in reciting it, they did not feel that they were breaking the commandment about gods. Why? Because Jesus shared the Father's deity.

To the Jews, the title *Christ* was particularly significant. It was the Greek word for the Hebrew term *Messiah*. Who is Jesus, the carpenter of Nazareth, the itinerant teacher and miracle worker? He is God's anointed prophet, priest, king, and wise man. He is the one to whom the prophets pointed, the son of David come to set his people free. He is the Savior to whom the whole Old Testament looks, the Son and Servant of God commissioned to bring salvation.

Lord and Christ—no description of Jesus can be accurate or adequate without these two titles—titles that tie him unbreakably to the person and program of God, whom he taught us to call Father.

The One Who Shares the Aims of God

The program of God is described in a brief but forceful phrase: "to deliver us from the present evil age . . . " (Gal. 1:4). Paul saw that the whole mood and tone of life was out of phase with God's purposes. Values were distorted; motives were perverted. Man was both victim and culprit in a world where sin was a way of life.

It was God's aim to do something about it. Jesus Christ came not only as one who bears the names of God, but as one who shares the aims of God. He "gave himself for our sins to deliver us from the present evil age, according to the will of our God and Father" (Gal. 1:4).

A rescue operation based on the forgiveness of sins—

that was God's aim. We are not innocent spectators in the game of sin; we are eager participants. We are not stunned bystanders at the site of the crime; we are accessories before, during, and after the fact.

Who is Jesus Christ? He is the one who shares God's aim of putting history right, by starting where history went wrong—with human sin.

He can set straight our *intellectual arrogance*, one of the symptoms of the present evil age. We think that our brainpower can solve all human problems. A colleague of mine at Fuller Theological Seminary is a distinguished American psychologist—a pioneer in the field of speech pathology, the study of the causes and cures of stuttering and other speech impediments. For years, as he carried on his research and trained more than one hundred Ph.D.s, he viewed man as a combination of brain and body, needing no help for anything beyond himself. Then Jesus Christ found him and taught him how weak and inadequate our best efforts are. Jesus rescued this professor from the present evil age with its intellectual arrogance and taught him lessons of humility and trust.

And Jesus can set straight our *moral corruption*, another symptom of the present evil age. A man shook my hand and said, "Four weeks ago I was producing sex films. Last night I wrote a hymn." An actor had come to his studio seeking a job. The actor had turned down an offer to work in sex films, with the simple response: "Thank you, I don't take that kind of job. I'm a Christian." For months that answer stuck in that film maker's mind. He became more and more troubled about the kind of films he was producing and their impact on society. Finally, he saw the actor in a restaurant, went over to him, and reminded him of the conversation months before. The actor took him to church, where Jesus Christ met him and changed his life. Jesus rescued him from the present evil age with its moral corruption and taught him to sing the praises of God.

Jesus can also set straight our *materialistic ambition,* a further symptom of the present evil age. By the time he was forty-two years old, another friend had achieved all his personal goals—a lovely wife, a fine family, a magnificent home, a prominent reputation as an eye surgeon, a lucrative practice. He loved art—paintings, etchings, lamps, vases, antiques. He scoured the catalogs and haunted the auctions. Painfully he found that each new acquisition brought him pleasure about as long as it took to unwrap it and hang it, or to place it on a table. Then his passion to *acquire* would flame up again, and he would be off to find his next purchase. One night his wife dragged him to church—an almost unprecedented experience for him. There the Bishop of Coventry, in town only for that service, leaned over the pulpit and spoke about his friend, the Savior. Jesus rescued that surgeon from the present evil age and taught him to love *persons* more than *things.*

Who is Jesus Christ? Superstar? Perhaps, but more. Who is Jesus Christ? Revolutionary folk hero? Maybe. But much more. Wise teacher? Yes. Wonder-worker? Of course, but a great deal more. (He may even have worn a mustache!)

He is Jesus *now.* Risen from the dead. He is Jesus now, lavishing upon us grace and peace—unqualified acceptance and unlimited wholeness. He is Jesus now, rescuing us from the arrogance, the corruption, the ambition of our evil age.

Who is Jesus Christ? In a sense that is a question that you and I do not need to answer. It has already been answered by our Lord himself and by his apostles: he is the one, the only one, who bears God's names and shares God's aims.

You and I need not decide who Jesus Christ is, because we have God's own word on that. But we *must* decide whether or not we will yield to his claims.

2

How Good
Is the Good News?

Galatians 1:6-17

*I am astonished that you are so quickly deserting him
who called you in the grace of Christ and turning to a
different gospel—not that there is another gospel, but
there are some who trouble you and want to pervert
the gospel of Christ. But even if we, or an angel from
heaven, should preach to you a gospel contrary to that
which we preached to you, let him be accursed. As we
have said before, so now I say again, If any one is
preaching to you a gospel contrary to that which you
received, let him be accursed.*

*Am I now seeking the favor of men, or of God? Or
am I trying to please men? If I were still pleasing men,
I should not be a servant of Christ.*

*For I would have you know, brethren, that the gospel
which was preached by me is not man's gospel. For I
did not receive it from man, nor was I taught it, but it
came through a revelation of Jesus Christ. For you have
heard of my former life in Judaism, how I persecuted
the church of God violently and tried to destroy it; and*

I advanced in Judaism beyond many of my own age among my people, so extremely zealous was I for the traditions of my fathers. But when he who had set me apart before I was born, and had called me through his grace, was pleased to reveal his Son to me, in order that I might preach him among the Gentiles, I did not confer with flesh and blood, nor did I go up to Jerusalem to those who were apostles before me, but I went away into Arabia; and again I returned to Damascus.

I could feel the excitement as they came into the airport. There were a dozen or so of them—kids from about ten to fourteen years of age. The youngsters looked excited; their sponsors looked apprehensive.

A couple of the kids sat next to me on the plane from Dayton to Chicago. Bouncing with enthusiasm, they told me what they were doing and why. "We are newspaper carriers for the *Kettering-Oakwood Times,*" they announced. "We have won a trip to Chicago for the weekend." They had worked hard and waited long. Now the day had arrived, and they were bursting with good news.

Good news—it comes in many forms. Since we know this, the questions naturally spring to mind, "What about the gospel? What makes it such good news? How good is the good news?"

The Gospel Is Good News Because It Happened

Perhaps we can discover just how good the good news of the gospel is by contrasting it with what it is not. The gospel is *not religious myth.* Take the Babylonian creation epic, for instance. It recounts the struggle of their great god Marduk to create the heavens and earth. *Struggle* is the right word, because, according to the Babylonians, Marduk had to slay a rival god before creation could take place. The carcass of the slain god was cut in two pieces—one of which became the great vault of heaven, the other the flat plain of earth. The gospel of Jesus Christ is not myth like this story. It is good news which really happened.

And the gospel is *not philosophical opinion.* A philosopher seeks to unravel the problems of human existence and to braid them together again in a way that makes sense out of as much of life's data as possible. What he ends with is measured judgment at best and foolish conjecture at worst. But the Christian gospel is not the distillation of a wise man's thinking. It is good news which really happened.

Again, the gospel is *not mystical vision.* The mystic meditates on the nature of God and hopes to be caught up in a religious experience that will lift him above the pain and toil of the world. But the gospel is not a brief episode of spiritual levitation. It is good news which really happened.

If the gospel were religious myth, it would have collapsed under the onslaughts of science. If the gospel were philosophical opinion, it would have been rendered passé by the reasonings of a subsequent philosopher. If the gospel were a mystical vision, it would have been called into question by the harsh realities of life. Did that experience really happen? Was it only a dream? How does being lifted above the pain and toil of life momentarily help me live amid that pain and toil permanently?

The good news that Jesus brought really happened.

It is *historical*. It took place at a date which can be
circled on a calendar. It occurred at a spot which can
be marked on a map. It centered in a man whose deeds
are logged in human archives.

In his definition of the gospel Paul made this plain:
"Now I would remind you, brethren, in what terms I
preached to you the gospel. . . . For I delivered to you
as of first importance what I also received, that Christ
died for our sins in accordance with the scriptures, that
he was buried, that he was raised on the third day in
accordance with the scriptures, and that he appeared to
Cephas, then to the twelve" (1 Cor. 15:1, 3–5). Jesus
really died and really rose again—this is the substance
of God's good news which Paul preached and by which
his hearers were saved if they truly believed. It is good
news because it actually happened.

Small wonder that Paul became impatient, even in-
dignant, when anyone tried to tamper with this basic
message. He left no doubt in the minds of his friends in
Galatia about the dangers of such tampering: "I am
astonished that you are so quickly deserting him who
called you in the grace of Christ and turning to a different gospel—not that there is another gospel, but
there are some who trouble you and want to pervert
the gospel of Christ" (Gal. 1:6–7).

With these strong words Paul warned both his
friends and his enemies against perverting the gospel.
It was the Judaizers whom he had in mind, those Jewish
Christians who taught that the good news of the gospel
was not sufficient for salvation. Circumcision, as a sym-
bol of obedience to law, had to be added to it.

To add to the gospel or to take away from the gospel
leaves you with no gospel—that was Paul's argument.

"But even if we, or an angel from heaven, should preach to you a gospel contrary to that which we preached to you, let him be accursed" (Gal. 1:8). And lest his hearers not believe their ears, Paul repeated the warning: "let him be accursed" (Gal. 1:9).

The message is more important than the messenger. It is a specific good news of what happened in history through Jesus Christ. No one dare change it on threat of damnation.

The Gospel Is Good News
Because God Made It Happen

Not all that happens in history is good news. The owner of the building in Times Square, New York City, where the news is flashed in lights to the pedestrians in the crowded intersection, has grown tired of bad news. He recently gave orders that nothing but good news is to be lettered out in his bright lights. He may have a hard time sending a continuous flow of news. So much of it tends to be bad. But not the gospel. It is good news because *God* made it happen.

The gospel is not a technological accomplishment, like the building of a gigantic dam. That is good news— good news of water conserved, of floods controlled, of recreation provided, of power generated. But it is human achievement, and no more.

The gospel is not a scientific breakthrough, like the discovery of the Salk vaccine for polio. That was good news—good news of disease defeated, of pain avoided, of anxiety averted, of epidemics eliminated. But it was human achievement, unable to touch the dark forces that paralyze the human spirit.

The gospel is not an artistic triumph, like the composition of Beethoven's Ninth Symphony. That was good news—good news of melody and harmony, of inspiration and excitement, of celebration and joy. But it was human achievement, unable to tune the heart to the eternal songs of God.

Building the dam, discovering the vaccine, writing the symphony—these are all examples of good news *because of* what man has done. The gospel is good news *in spite of* what man has done. It is God's good work when man has done his worst.

It is good news like the gentle voice of a doctor assuring a person that he or she will recover from a foolish overdose of drugs. Good news *in spite of* what the person had done. It is good news like the comforting report that the wallet carelessly lost has been recovered with cash and credit cards intact. Good news *in spite of* what the person deserved.

At heart, the gospel is good news about God. God, who could have dealt with us in judgment, has offered grace and peace (Gal. 1:3). God, who could have abandoned us to our own rebellion, willed that Jesus should rescue us from the present evil age (Gal. 1:4). God, who could have left us to wander in our lostness, sent special messages through the Apostle Paul to tell us of his love (Gal. 1:12). God, who sent his Son with the good news, also saw to it that Paul was especially called and equipped to understand and pass on the good news to us (Gal. 1:13–17).

God made it happen—this good news. It is his doing. The crucifixion and resurrection were his work, to make pardon possible. And the conversion and commissioning of the apostle were his work, to make sure that the news was relayed accurately and demonstrated dramatically.

Paul was not seeking the good news. It found him—found him as a devout, zealous, well-trained Jew living to destroy the church of God. Nothing in his background caused him to dream up this good news. Nothing after his conversion caused him to concoct it. No rabbi before Christ met him, and no apostle after Christ met him, could account for Paul's message. It was plainly and simply a gift of God, revealed by the risen Christ on the road to Damascus and interpreted by the Holy Spirit to him in the Arabian desert, where Paul remained for about three years before his public ministry began.

The Gospel Is Good News Which God Made Happen for Us

How good is the good news? What makes it good news? It *happened* in history. It is a fact that we can count on. And it is more. It is what *God* made happen in spite of what we had done and deserved. But that is not all. It is especially good news—God's gospel—because it is good news which he made happen *for us*.

Most good news is selective. It brings joy to some and leaves others empty. A biochemist in Pasadena wins a Nobel prize. What is good news for him leaves dozens of biochemists throughout the world dissatisfied. A political candidate savors the sweet taste of victory in one downtown hotel, while across the street his opponent chokes back the tears of defeat. After every ball game, what is good news in one locker room is bitter loss in the other.

Not so with the gospel of Christ. It is not a word to the intellectual alone, to the popular alone, to the strong and talented alone. It is not a word for the elite alone. It is for all of us.

In a sense, Paul was Exhibit A of the inclusive nature of the good news. "For you have heard of my former life in Judaism, how I persecuted the church of God violently and tried to destroy it" (Gal. 1:13). How good is the good news? Paul's answer was personal: it is good enough to include a bigotted persecutor whose life's aim was to wipe out the Church.

And the Galatians themselves were Exhibit B. Despite their confusion about the gospel, despite their temptation to change, despite their flirtation with the false teachings of the Judaizers, the gospel was still good news to them and for them. In a calm and confident voice over the din of their uncertainty, it reminded them of the love and grace of God which alone make salvation a reality.

How good is the good news? It is good enough to change a persecutor on the way to his cruelest assignment—to bring Christians from Damascus to Jerusalem in chains. How good is the good news? It is good enough to steady halting and faltering believers in danger of seduction and betrayal.

How good is the good news? It is good enough still to be good when life's other reports turn bad. In suffering, it offers grace and peace. In temptation, it promises rescue. It is the news of freedom to a slave, the news of adoption to an orphan, the news of pardon to a convict.

How good is the good news? Good enough to let us

take all that life sends and still have joy. It has revealed to us the loving Son of God (Gal. 1:16). That revelation carries with it enough good news to last a lifetime. And beyond!

3

How Can I Have the Courage of My Convictions?

Galatians 1:15-2:10

But when he who had set me apart before I was born, and had called me through his grace, was pleased to reveal his Son to me, in order that I might preach him among the Gentiles, I did not confer with flesh and blood, nor did I go up to Jerusalem to those who were apostles before me, but I went away into Arabia; and again I returned to Damascus.

Then after three years I went up to Jerusalem to visit Cephas, and remained with him fifteen days. But I saw none of the other aspostles except James the Lord's brother. (In what I am writing to you, before God, I do not lie!) Then I went into the regions of Syria and Cilicia. And I was still not known by sight to the churches of Christ in Judea; they only heard it said, "He who once persecuted us is now preaching the faith he once tried to destroy." And they glorified God because of me.

Then after fourteen years I went up again to Jerusalem with Barnabas, taking Titus along with me. I went up by revelation; and I laid before them (but privately before those who were of repute) the gospel which I preach among the Gentiles; lest somehow I should be running or had run in vain. But even Titus, who was with me, was not compelled to be circumcised, though he was a Greek. But because of false brethren secretly brought in, who slipped in to spy out our freedom which we have in Christ Jesus, that they might bring us into bondage—to them we did not yield submission even for a moment, that the truth of the gospel might be preserved for you. And from those who were reputed to be something (what they were makes no difference to me; God shows no partiality)—those, I say, who were of repute added nothing to me; but on the contrary, when they saw that I had been entrusted with the gospel to the uncircumcised, just as Peter had been entrusted with the gospel to the circumcised (for he who worked through Peter for the mission to the circumcised worked through me also for the Gentiles), and when they perceived the grace that was given to me, James and Cephas and John, who were reputed to be pillars, gave to me and Barnabas the right hand of fellowship, that we should go to the Gentiles and they to the circumcised; only they would have us remember the poor, which very thing I was eager to do.

Without courage there can be no freedom. Courage is part of that eternal vigilance which is the price of liberty.

The kings of the east swooped down on Sodom and snatched Lot as a prisoner. With 318 men and a great deal of courage, Abraham set out to win Lot's freedom.

The Pharaoh of Egypt tried to break the backs of the Israelites by a harsh conspiracy of oppression and genocide. With his brother Aaron, a wondrous rod, and a full measure of courage, Moses sought freedom for his people.

The Canaanites, under King Jabin, used iron chariots to terrorize the tribes of Israel for twenty years. With ten thousand troops from Zebulon and Naphtali, Deborah and Barak found courage to challenge the Canaanites on the banks of the river Kishon, and to win a forty-year span of freedom for the tribes.

The illustrations could be multiplied. Abraham Lincoln's courage to issue the Emancipation Proclamation in 1863 and the courage of the United States Supreme Court to desegregate our school systems in 1954 would be just two links in a chain of more modern examples that could also include freedom fighters in Hungary and Czechoslovakia.

Freedom takes courage, because freedom is not the usual state in which human beings find themselves. Left to our own devices, we almost always end up in some form of slavery. Sin works that way. "Truly, truly, I say to you, every one who commits sin is a slave to sin" (John 8:34). These words of Jesus capture a basic principle: sin wars against freedom and usually wins.

Our sinfulness leads us into slavery to sin. But it does more. It makes us eager not only to enslave others, but also to be enslaved ourselves. What are totalitarian governments but systems of slavery, where personal free-

doms are traded for economic and social security. Half
of the world's population right now has made that trade.
Though force has often been used to bring about and
to maintain such political structures, most people have
only themselves to blame for submitting so willingly to
the systems which serve as captors. They have not yet
been willing to muster the courage that it takes to win
their freedom and to live with its uncertainties and
risks.

Courage is not merely mindless rebellion; nor is it
spineless conformity. It is something different. It is the
will to discover what is right, and then to live for what
is right, even at high personal cost.

Paul's Example of Courage

Set free from the slavery of his former life, emanci-
pated from the bonds of his dependence on law, the
Apostle Paul time and time again revealed the courage
needed to assure the freedom of his spiritual followers.
From his examples of courage, especially in the letter to
the Galatians, we can learn lessons of courage in our
own struggles for freedom.

Paul's example tells us that courage alone is not
enough. Courage, to produce strength, conviction, and
change, must be linked to other experiences. For instance, courage can readily turn to brashness if it is not
guided and supported by *knowledge*.

The challenge to Paul's courage was not a simple one.
He had faced opposition, and even persecution, many
times and acquitted himself well. In the circumstances
that he recounted to the Galatians he was not facing a
hostile crowd in a pagan marketplace; he was not de-

bating with irate Jews in an Asian synagogue. He was face to face with leaders of the Jerusalem church; he was on the edge of conflict with the other apostles. To *know* what he believed and what he should do was essential in that situation.

How could he be sure? Where did his knowledge come from? Here is the answer to those questions in Paul's own words: "But when he who had set me apart before I was born, and had called me through his grace, was pleased to reveal his Son to me, in order that I might preach him among the Gentiles, I did not confer with flesh and blood, nor did I go up to Jerusalem to those who were apostles before me, but I went away into Arabia; and again I returned to Damascus" (Gal. 1:15–17).

"Was pleased to reveal his Son to me" is the key clause. Paul's knowledge that bolstered his courage was not based on casual hearsay. It was not a rumor circulated in back corridors. It was not even the ponderous opinion of a learned sage. The revelation of God was the foundation of his courage. He had met the Son of God; he had heard the good news of God; he had been commissioned for the mission of God to the Gentiles. When the pressure was on him to compromise his convictions, to force his Gentile friend Titus to be circumcised, he drew courage from this knowledge.

His courage was refined by his *patience*. "Nor did I go up to Jerusalem to those who were apostles before me, but I went away into Arabia; and again I returned to Damascus" (Gal. 1:17). What was Paul doing in Arabia? Preaching? Perhaps, but nowhere did he make mention of any ministry there. Almost always his missions were to the urban centers of the Mediterranean. It does not seem likely that he would have begun his career by preaching to the Bedouin tribes scattered across the Arabian desert.

What was Paul doing in Arabia? Probably meditating. His entire life had been changed; his goals were about to be redirected. That vast knowledge of the Scriptures and Jewish tradition garnered in his home and refined in his study with the master rabbi, Gamaliel, had to be reevaluated and reinterpreted.

All of this took time. As Moses had forty years of desert life in preparation for his mission, as David spent months in the wilderness as a fugitive from Saul's fury, as Elijah needed to regain his strength after the contests with Baal's prophets on Carmel, as John the Baptist contemplated the coming Kingdom, and as Jesus was readied for his ministry by temptation—both in the rough Judean wastelands—so the Apostle Paul was assigned to Arabia to bask in the sun of his newfound faith.

Patient contemplation was added to the dramatic revelation. Together, the contemplation and the revelation reinforced his courage. He needed no instruction from the other apostles; he needed no affirmation from the Jerusalem church. His knowledge of the gospel, patiently tested in the solitude of Arabia, built up his fortitude. He knew where he had to stand, and stand he did: "But even Titus, who was with me [on a trip to Jerusalem fourteen years after Paul's conversion], was not compelled to be circumcised, though he was a Greek. But because of false brethren secretly brought in, who slipped in to spy out our freedom which we

have in Christ Jesus, that they might bring us into
bondage—to them we did not yield submission even for
a moment, that the truth of the gospel might be preserved for you" (Gal. 2:3–5).

False brethren—we do not know who they were.
Paul does not dignify them with a more ample description. Apparently, they were Jews who pretended to be
Christians in order to infiltrate (notice the *spy* vocabu-
lary Paul used) Christian ranks and to provoke either
compromise or division.

Steeped in the gospel, Paul realized what their game
was and refused to go along with it. He had circumcised
Timothy because his mother and grandmother were
Jewish. But with Titus the case was different. Titus was
Greek. To allow him to be circumcised would have sent
a message around the Gentile world—a message that said
that the gospel was not enough, that circumcision and
law must be added to the gospel for salvation to take
place.

In digging his heels in at this issue, Paul showed that
his courage was demonstrated in his *independence*. He
refused to go along with the ploys of the spying false
brethren. If this refusal meant standing alone, so be it.
Nothing in the text suggests that Paul gained any aid or
comfort from the other apostles. His courage to resist
did not come from them.

Yet his independence was not just personal stubbornness. Paul's motive was the welfare of the gentile
Church—and, therefore, of the whole Church, for
when one part of the body suffers, the whole Church
shares the pain.

Paul was not pushy with his own power. He was not

grasping after prestige or recognition. The truth of the gospel was at stake. Christian freedom was on the block. The false brethren had one aim—"that they might bring us into bondage." The courageous Apostle had one motivation—"that the truth of the gospel might be preserved for you."

The most amazing thing about this example of courage is that it resulted in *fellowship:* "And when they perceived the grace that was given to me, James and Cephas [Peter] and John, who were reputed to be pillars, gave to me and Barnabas the right hand of fellowship, that we should go to the Gentiles and they to the circumcised" (Gal. 2:9).

Paul's courage was vindicated. Because he had his facts right and weighed them thoroughly, and because his motives were not selfish, he was able to bridge the differences of attitude, background, and culture, and to preserve the unity of the Church. That right hand of fellowship, when the great Jerusalem worthies—Peter, James, John, the intimate friends of Jesus—reached out in oneness with the Apostle to the heathen world, may have been history's most monumental handshake.

Without it, we might have had two Churches. And two Churches at that juncture might have set up splits and rifts which could have toppled the Church to dust. Jesus had pledged that "the powers of death shall not prevail against" the Church (Matt. 16:18). A loving handclasp in Jerusalem proved to be one of the ways in which Jesus fulfilled that pledge.

Our Response to Paul's Example

How can I have the courage of my convictions?

Paul's account is so clear that we need only to sketch the ways in which we may respond to his example.

How can I have the courage of my convictions? By *making sure I have the right information.* How many causes have been hurt, how many persons have been wounded by rash decisions based on inadequate knowledge?

We do not have the bright flashes of a meeting with Christ on the road to Damascus. We have something even better—the full revelation of God in the Scriptures.

Our task—before we take sides in a major issue—is to make sure that we know as much as possible of what the Bible says. Where the Bible speaks clearly, we can afford to take a strong stand; where it does not, we should be cautioned to speak with humility.

How can I have the courage of my convictions? By *reflecting before I act.* We all need our Arabias, our time and opportunity to weigh issues and ponder implications. This is particularly true if the action to be taken is life-changing. A new job? A distant move? A commitment to marriage? A confrontation with a pastor? A change of churches? Take time. The old proverb "Act in haste, repent in leisure" is yet true. Pray about your course of action until you are sure that you know what you are doing and that you are doing it for the right reasons.

How can I have the courage of my convictions? By *holding firm when I am convinced.* This is especially true in matters that are crucial to our faith. There can be lots of give, lots of flexibility in matters of opinion, taste or culture. Paul was willing to "become all things

to all men, that I might by all means save some" (1 Cor.
9:22). But where the truth of the gospel, the unity of
the Church, or the success of the Christian mission was
on the line, no compromise was possible.

How can I have the courage of my convictions? By
seeking fellowship even when I disagree. Where fellow
Christians are involved, we may have to differ on issues
while still affirming that the people we disagree with
are still our brothers and sisters, with their place in
Christ's Body and their mission in Christ's Church.

Amiable disagreement, brotherly confrontation is not
a frequent commodity among God's people. And we
are the poorer, because our differences so often lead to
divisions.

True Christian courage works for reconciliation,
though at times reconciliation may be beyond our reach.
We see stubbornness on every hand; compromise is for
sale by the ton. But *courage*—that is something else. Its
rarity makes us treasure Paul's example. Its worth—as
the price of true freedom—makes us look to our response.

4

Whom Can I
Call My Brother?

Galatians 2:11-21

*But when Cephas came to Antioch I opposed him to
his face, because he stood condemned. For before certain men came from James, he ate with the Gentiles;
but when they came he drew back and separated himself, fearing the circumcision party. And with him the
rest of the Jews acted insincerely, so that even Barnabas
was carried away by their insincerity. But when I saw
that they were not straightforward about the truth of
the gospel, I said to Cephas before them all, "If you,
though a Jew, live like a Gentile and not like a Jew,
how can you compel the Gentiles to live like Jews?"
We ourselves, who are Jews by birth and not Gentile
sinners, yet who know that a man is not justified by
works of the law but through faith in Jesus Christ, even
we have believed in Christ Jesus, in order to be justified
by faith in Christ, and not by works of the law, because
by works of the law shall no one be justified. But if, in
our endeavor to be justified in Christ, we ourselves were
found to be sinners, is Christ then an agent of sin? Cer-*

tainly not! But if I build up again those things which I tore down, then I prove myself a transgressor. For I through the law died to the law, that I might live to God. I have been crucified with Christ; it is no longer I who live, but Christ who lives in me; and the life I now live in the flesh I live by faith in the Son of God, who loved me and gave himself for me. I do not nullify the grace of God; for if justification were through the law, then Christ died to no purpose.

The church page in the Saturday newspaper started me pondering over the problem once again. It listed the various services in our community—denomination by denomination, congregation by congregation.

My problem was not how to understand the sermon titles, although I admit that some of them sounded intriguing enough to make me want to visit several churches on the same Sunday morning. My problem was not the number of congregations listed. I think there should be churches in every neighborhood. Often a smaller congregation offers an intimacy of fellowship and an opportunity for service not found in large congregations, where so many members are tempted to be mere spectators.

My problem was not the diversity of denominations represented on that church page. I realize that denominations often have legitimate differences in their understanding of the Scriptures—differences in views of baptism or ordination or church government. The various denominations, with their differing styles of liturgy and worship, appeal to different tastes. Besides, many of

the denominational differences in the United States re-
flect the impact of historical events, like the Reforma-
tion, which divided the churches in Europe: Lutherans
in Germany and Scandinavia, Anglicans in England,
Presbyterians in Scotland, Switzerland, Holland, and
parts of France. These differences and others were ex-
ported to the New World with the hosts of immigrants
who settled here in the past three centuries. This historical process has been used by God to reach, for his
Kingdom, numbers of people of differing intellectual,
social, and economic levels. It would prove difficult to
change these historical realities and the impression they
have made on the Church, even if we were to determine
that it would be desirable.

When I have said all this, my problem remains. The
multiplicity of congregations I can accept. The variety
of denominations I can understand. What troubles me
is something else.

Most simply put, it is this: which of those churches
belong to me? Whom of their members can I call my
brother? When I read the church page I need a program to tell the players from the spectators. Which of
those congregations are part of God's team doing his
will in the world, and which are not?

Jesus prepared us for this problem. He reminded us
that the Church was not the world and that the world
was not the Church. A distinction must be made between the world and the Church. "They are not of the
world," he said of the apostles who were the nucleus of
his newborn Church, "even as I am not of the world"
(John 17:16). Jesus also warned us that not all who
claim to follow him really do: "Not every one who
says to me, 'Lord, Lord,' shall enter the kingdom of

heaven, but he who does the will of my Father who is in heaven" (Matt. 7:21).

The church page, then, may contain the listings of churches which are really part of the world and not of the Church. Their pastors and congregations may be calling "Lord, Lord," without really belonging to him. Whom can I call my brother? How do I know which of these enterprises and which people within them are part of Christ's true Church?

To get at the answers to those questions we have to raise another question—another even more *basic* question: What is it that makes a person a Christian? Surprisingly, Christ's people had trouble with that question right from the beginning. It was to answer that question—what makes a person a Christian?—that Paul, Christ's special messenger, wrote his letter to the Galatians.

In the first two chapters of the letter Paul was struggling to get two points across: first, the good news of the gospel is that men and women are saved by trusting in Christ's grace and not by their own efforts to keep the Old Testament law; second, as an official interpreter of the gospel, Paul proclaimed a message which is utterly trustworthy in its authority.

Paul's argument about his authority has run like this. Neither the message that he preached nor his commission to preach was of human origin. His calling and his gospel came from Christ himself (Gal. 1:1, 11–12). Nothing in his background before Christ conquered him on the Damascus road equipped him to preach the word of grace, because his whole life had been dedicated to Jewish law (Gal. 1:13–14). Even after his conversion, it was three years before he conferred with any of the other apostles, and then only for a fifteen-day period—hardly time enough for them to give him thorough instruction. When he did go to Jerusalem for a longer visit years later, his authority as an apostle was acknowledged by Peter, James, and John. In fact, Paul's conviction that his gentile associate Titus should not submit to circumcision was finally upheld by the other leaders, despite a lot of pressure from Jewish Christians (Gal. 1:15–2:10).

Then Paul brought his argument about his office and his dependability to a strong conclusion with a telling piece of evidence: in a moment of conflict between Paul and Peter, it was Paul, and not Peter, who showed himself to be the authoritative teacher (Gal. 2:11–21). That controversy with Peter also gave Paul the opportunity to reassure his readers about the nature of the gospel, and, along the way, to help us answer our question: Whom can I call my brother or my sister?

Peter's Breach of Brotherhood

Here is Paul's account of the conflict: "But when Cephas [that is Peter's Aramaic name, which means 'rock'] came to Antioch I opposed him to his face, because he stood condemned. For before certain men came from James, he ate with the Gentiles; but when they came he drew back and separated himself, fearing the circumcision party" (Gal. 2:11–12).

Paul challenged Peter's action because Peter *knew better*. Years before, the Lord himself had spoken to Peter in a vision and instructed him to change his attitude toward believers who were Gentiles. Peter's lifelong prejudice had been corrected by a word from the risen Christ (Acts 10:9–16). Immediately Peter had put that lesson into practice in the house of Cornelius, a Roman army officer. These were Peter's own words: "You yourselves know how unlawful it is for a Jew to associate with or to visit any one of another nation; but God has shown me that I should not call any man common or unclean. So when I was sent for, I came without objection . . ." (Acts 10:28–29).

And for years Peter had followed the practice of eating with Gentile Christians whenever he had been with them. He had known what Christian fellowship really was. He had been willing to let all barriers of race and culture be leveled by the gospel. Then at Antioch, the headquarters of the gentile church, Peter went back to his old ways and refused to sit at the table with gentiles.

Paul challenged Peter's action because Peter was *doing it for the wrong reason*. Peter's sudden change of practice was not due to a fresh revelation from God, a new insight from the Scriptures, or a strong conviction of his conscience. Peter pulled back from fellowship with Gentiles for one wrong reason: he was afraid of the circumcision party. One fold for Christ's sheep and one gate to that sheepfold, so all Christians taught. But the quarrel came over the definition of that one gate. The circumcision party held that the gate was a Jewish gate and that circumcision was the key to it. No one could be a full-fledged Christian who did not first become a Jew. An influential group they were, backed by the power and prestige of many of the Christian leaders of Jerusalem. Peter apparently feared that they would undermine his influence and hurt his reputation if he did not go along with their persuasions.

Paul challenged Peter because *Peter's conduct harmed the Church.* "And with him the rest of the Jews acted insincerely, so that even Barnabas was carried away by their insincerity" (Gal. 2:13). What else would you expect? What the distinguished leader from Jerusalem did, other Jewish Christians would do as well. What the stalwart companion of Jesus would practice would be readily followed even by Paul's close friend and coworker, Barnabas.

Probably what harmed the Church most in Peter's hypocritical conduct was that the Gentiles felt that they were second class. Somehow Christ's love for them was not so strong; somehow God's grace to them was not so great. God's best bread went to the Jews, and the Gentiles tagged along hoping for some crumbs; God's best wine went to the circumcised, and the uncircumcised had to content themselves with the dregs.

Separate tables for eating meant that Jewish Christians and Gentile Christians no longer took communion together. The love feast where those early Christians shared a meal and then partook of the bread and wine of holy communion became a sign of separateness, not fellowship. The ark of salvation sailed along with the circumcised Christians in the first class section, while the uncircumcised Christians traveled in steerage. And Peter had been responsible for this breach of brotherhood.

Paul's Call to Brotherhood

Paul pointed out Peter's inconsistency. Ever since

that vision of the unclean animals and the meeting with Cornelius, Peter had been living like a Gentile, enjoying food and fellowship at gentile tables. Now he was asking Gentiles to live like Jews.

But Peter's conduct was more inconsistent than that. Peter was a Jew. But his race had not saved him. Peter was a circumcised Jew, but his religious devotion had not saved him. As Paul argued, it is faith and only faith that God asks of both Jew and Gentile: ". . . even we [circumcised Jews] have believed in Christ Jesus, in order to be justified by faith in Christ, and not by works of the law, because by works of the law shall no one [Jew or Gentile] be justified" (Gal. 2:16).

Paul warned Peter against the worst sin of all. Eating with Gentiles was not a sin. But Peter was in danger of committing a terrifying sin. "But if I build up again those things which I tore down, then I prove myself a transgressor" (Gal. 2:18). To try to be saved by law, to rebuild the scaffold of human works, to use circumcision as a ladder to heaven—that is the real transgression. To trust in law is to say to Christ, "You are not the Savior. I am. I do not need your help. I can save myself."

To trust in human effort, including religious effort, for salvation is to declare the death of Christ history's greatest waste: "I do not nullify the grace of God; for if justification were through the law, then Christ died to no purpose" (Gal. 2:21).

Paul taught Peter a lesson of faith. We must not try to pump life into dead works. We live by dying—dying to all our own claims to merit, to honor, to goodness. Paul's words are blunt: "I have been crucified with

Christ." In other words, when he died, I died—died to law, died to circumcision, died to all my endeavors to save myself.

"It is no longer I who live, but Christ who lives in me." A radically different life this is, not motivated by pride, not sensitive to prestige, not afraid of pressures. Christ is my Savior. I live secure in him.

"And the life I now live in the flesh I live by faith in the Son of God, who loved me and gave himself for me" (Gal. 2:20). Not the harsh cut of circumcision, but the tender love of Christ is our hope for salvation. We do not *try* to please God; we *trust* because he has already been pleased with Christ.

The badge of brotherhood—circumcision? Not at all. The bond of fellowship—loyalty to law? Not now.

Whom shall I call my brother or my sister? Those who share my faith in the crucified and risen Christ.

What makes persons Christian? Not a matching of color, but a meeting at the cross. Not an expression of culture, but an experience of crucifixion.

Look at the church page of that Saturday newspaper and choose your own church by the standards of doctrine and the patterns of government that seem most biblical to you. But let your arms of fellowship be open to all who confess the Lord Jesus Christ as Son of God and Savior.

Brotherhood is not a product of race, dress, style, language, education, wealth, taste. It is the costly gift of God's grace to all who meet him and each other at the cross of Christ.

1. It takes stupidity to miss the pt. So obvious a sign of God's vote or way of path

2. God has always ___ the same way fr man: faith. It's the true religion! Abraham is not a law-abider, but a faith exhibitor,

Here well laid out in 3 main outline parts of idea of this The only true religion is trust in God that shields & preserves.

3. Built by man's efforts as insurance.
Not newly because Moses said 'curse of law' – what is it? It is the guilt – which man incurs; suffers. It's my curse! Conscience, we'd say, which law reveals – but you cannot forgive your own guilt – against God. He alone can do that. He declares forgiveness. It's something we receive.

Why Do I Need to Have Faith?

Galatians 3:1-14

O foolish Galatians! Who has bewitched you, before whose eyes Jesus Christ was publicly portrayed as crucified? Let me ask you only this: Did you receive the Spirit by works of the law, or by hearing with faith? Are you so foolish? Having begun with the Spirit, are you now ending with the flesh? Did you experience so many things in vain?—if it really is in vain. Does he who supplies the Spirit to you and works miracles among you do so by works of the law, or by hearing with faith?

Thus Abraham "believed God, and it was reckoned to him as righteousness." So you see that it is men of faith who are the sons of Abraham. And the scripture, foreseeing that God would justify the Gentiles by faith, preached the gospel beforehand to Abraham, saying, "In you shall all the nations be blessed." So then, those who are men of faith are blessed with Abraham who had faith.

For all who rely on works of the law are under a

51

curse; for it is written, "Cursed be every one who does not abide by all things written in the book of the law, and do them." Now it is evident that no man is justified before God by the law; for "He who through faith is righteous shall live"; but the law does not rest on faith, for "He who does them shall live by them." Christ redeemed us from the curse of the law, having become a curse for us—for it is written, "Cursed be every one who hangs on a tree"—that in Christ Jesus the blessing of Abraham might come upon the Gentiles, that we might receive the promise of the Spirit through faith.

How do you respond to someone who has done you a favor? You probably cannot answer that question without further information. You will want to ask me some questions before you give your answer.

Questions like these. What kind of favor are you talking about? Who did the favor for me? What kind of commitment did the favor entail?

To a waitress or a porter who has done us a special favor, we usually respond with a tip. Ten, fifteen, twenty percent of the bill we leave for them because they have been especially considerate of us.

Most favors involve a commitment limited in time and energy. The porter carries our bags from the car to the baggage counter and duly labels them for our destination. He does not offer to paint our house or even to wash our car. His commitment is a specific one. He helps us cordially and efficiently, but only to the limits required by his particular assignment. And our commitment to him is likewise limited—twenty-five to fifty cents per bag, or a little more if they are unusually bulky or if he has to carry them far.

Some favors involve a much more substantial commitment. The example that rushes to mind is a mother's commitment to a newborn baby. Her ear is always tuned to hear her baby's call. Her time is at her baby's service: feedings at 10:00 P.M. and 2:00 A.M. and changings in between. Washing and ironing and straightening up, holding and cuddling and kissing the hurts, smiling and listening and teaching new words, the mother commits herself with very little reserve to her young one's needs.

What is adequate response to that kind of commitment? A tip? A thank you note? A dozen roses? These may be suitable expressions of thanks for some favors, but not for those long years when we were the center of our parents' lives. The ancient commandment summons us to *honor* father and mother. No other response is appropriate. We are to affirm their worth, to acknowledge their dignity, to reciprocate their care. This lifelong honoring, this pledge of permanent loyalty is all we can do to pay tribute to what our parents mean. Anything less is insulting tokenism.

A porter's favor gets one kind of response. A mother's favor gets another. The responses must be as different as the commitments involved. Now let us take this a step further. What if it is God who has rendered the favor, and what if the favor is the gift of his Son?

Think first of *who made the commitment*. The Lord of the universe is paying attention to us. The King of heaven is calling us by name. Can you remember how you felt when the principal of your elementary school

first spoke to you by name? Suddenly you stood a bit
taller. You had been singled out, recognized—I hope it
was not for disciplinary reasons—by the head of the
school. Lots of people knew your name—your family,
your neighbors, your Sunday school teacher, the grocer
at the corner. But this time it was the principal. And
that was different. She was an important person. Even
your teacher looked up to her. Yet she had called you
by name. Recapture that feeling, multiply it by infinity,
and you can gain some idea of what it means to have
God commit himself to us.

Think next of *the kind of commitment God has
made.* The best summary of it is found in these familiar
words: "For God so loved the world that he gave his
only Son, that whoever believes in him should not per-
ish but have eternal life" (John 3:16).

What motive prompted the commitment? Not personal gain, not selfish satisfaction, but *love. Our* needs
were the focus of God's concern.

How did he express that commitment? By signals of
thunder and lightning? By angels commissioned to en-
courage our hearts? No, by sending and, more than by
sending, by *giving* his Son. God went the full length in
responding to our needs.

What was the purpose of his commitment? Not to
use us as puppets or robots, not to exploit our weakness,
but to give us *life.* What we had no power to give ourselves, God's grace brought to us in abundant measure.

To whom was it that God made this commitment of
life-bringing love? Was it to the heavens that declare
his glory? Was it to the angels who are ministers of his

will? No, it was to the *world* that had set its face against him. "But God shows his love for us in that while we were yet sinners Christ died for us" (Rom. 5:8).

The Lord of the universe has made a commitment to us; and his commitment is total. These two points lead us back to our initial question: how do you respond to someone who has done you a favor? Or to rephrase the question in terms of our present discussion, How do you respond to the Father in heaven who has done you the favor of sending his Son to die for you?

Because it is *God* that has done the favor, we must look carefully to our response. Can we give money to the one who already owns the cattle on a thousand hills? Can we offer the feeble efforts of our hands to the one whose word created everything, including those hands? Quite the opposite. Because it is God who has done us the favor, our response must be to renounce all of our efforts to buy or to merit our own salvation.

God's favor is beyond price because it included the death of his Son. God spared nothing in his effort to bring us from darkness to light, from death to life. He did not even spare his own Son. His commitment was total.

Because his commitment was *total*, ours cannot be *token*. Nothing short of a full pledge of loyalty, nothing short of a promise of wholehearted allegiance, will do.

This is where faith comes in. Why do I need to have faith? Because faith is both a renunciation of my own fruitless attempts to please God and a response of my whole self to God's unreserved demonstration of love.

On his cross Christ "loved me and gave himself for me" (Gal. 2:20). By my faith I love him and give myself to him.

By Faith We Receive God's Spirit

In the first two chapters of Galatians, Paul braided together two skeins of thought: (1) his message had authority because Christ himself revealed it to him; (2) the gospel, which is the heart of his message, declares that God has offered salvation freely through Christ without any connection with law. In the last four chapters of the letter, Paul brought the latter strand into prominence. The good news—with its gracious announcement of freedom to all who believe—is the thread which binds the rest of the epistle together.

The Galatians needed to see this. They had come close to missing the whole point of what God had done through Jesus. Paul spoke strongly to them: "O foolish Galatians! Who has bewitched you, before whose eyes Jesus Christ was publicly portrayed as crucified?" (Gal. 3:1). Their problem was not ignorance. The crucifixion and its meaning for salvation had been declared as openly among the Galatians as though it had been blazoned from a billboard. Paul, with some sarcasm, raised the possibility that they had been hexed by a sorcerer so erratic had been their behavior.

The death of Jesus and its life-bringing power they had known. And the appropriate response of faith they had experienced. Paul reminded them of this in stinging questions: "Did you receive the Spirit by works of the law, or by hearing with faith? . . . Having begun with the Spirit, are you now ending with the flesh? Did you experience so many things in vain? . . . Does he who supplies the Spirit to you and works miracles among you do so by works of the law, or by hearing with faith?" (Gal. 3:2–5).

Those questions prompted their own answers. To back away from faith as the proper response to God would be to spurn the whole experience that had changed their lives.

By faith they had received God's Spirit. Their conversion transformed their way of living from fleshly to spiritual endeavor. In other words, they had begun to live in dependence on God's Spirit. They counted on him to see them through their suffering; they trusted him to bring maturity to their living; they rested in him for their assurance of life everlasting; they believed in him for power to cope with the problems of sin and sickness.

And their trust had not been in vain. The Spirit had done and was doing his work among them. Yet they were in danger of abandoning a life of faith for a life of law, which would be no life at all, because it would cut them off from the power of the Spirit who had brought life in the first place.

By Faith We Become Abraham's Children

Not working, but believing, was what had saved the Galatians. And this was not a new pattern. God had worked with Abraham the same way twenty centuries before.

What about Abraham had pleased God? Was it his personal integrity? No, Genesis is frank about the man's faults. Was it his perfect obedience? No, more than once we are told that Abraham took matters into his own hands. Was it his circumcision? No, circumcision was only the badge of something deeper—his loyalty to God, his commitment to him. Paul quoted the appropriate passage: "Thus Abraham 'believed God, and it was reckoned to him as righteousness'" (Gal. 3:6 from Gen. 15:6).

The false teachers, who were trying to distract the Galatian Christians from faith to works, from grace to law, from Spirit to flesh, had undoubtedly boasted that their ancestry went back to Abraham. They claimed him as their father. Not so, said Paul. God counted Abraham as a righteous man, as a true worshiper, not because he began the practice of circumcision but because he blazed the trail of faith. Those who respond to God's favor by believing God are the true children of Abraham, heirs of the blessings of life and liberty that God promised to him (Gal. 3:7-9).

3. By Faith We Escape the Curse of the Law

Faith, like Abraham's faith, brings blessing. Paul drove that principle home. But to make complete his picture of why we need to have faith, Paul had to add a shocking contrast: if faith brings blessing, law carries a curse. "... 'Cursed be every one who does not abide by all things written in the book of the law, and do them'" (Gal. 3:10 from Deut. 27:26), is the blunt text that Paul cited.

The law must be seen as a whole. A person cannot pick and choose the sections he will obey. He cannot cling to some commands and spurn others. To live by law means to live by the *whole* law—or else! As one

spot of jelly soils a tablecloth, as one nail hole flattens
a tire, so one broken command brings the whole law
tumbling down on us in judgment. That is the way the
law works.

Faith, on the other hand, sees that Christ bore the
brunt of God's law for us. Its oppressive weight, its
harsh curse, hung on him as he hung on the cross for
us: "Christ redeemed us from the curse of the law,
having become a curse for us . . ." (Gal. 3:13).

Why do I need to have faith? Because faith is the
only commitment suitable as a reply to God's message
of grace. The mighty God has poured out his all-
embracing love. What can I do but declare my total
dependence on him? What can I do but affirm my full
allegiance to him? What can I do but confess my whole
love for him?

When I do, God's Spirit, who has helped me make
this commitment, comes into my life with blessing and
power. God's favor does not stop with the cross; it
extends to where we live and suffer. He himself comes
to us in his Spirit.

When I do believe in God, I am linked to a great
family of faith, a family whose earthly father was Abraham. More than that, I am loosed from the burden of
trying to please God by compliance to his law.

When I believe God, I read myself into the story
of God's love. I hear the story with faith, as Paul
described it (Gal. 3:2, 5). I say, "Thank you, Lord,
for the favor you did for me." But I say more. I say,
"Take my person, Lord, as a loving gift. I can do
nothing else for the one who loved me and gave himself for me."

6

Why Did God Give the Law?

Galatians 3:15-29

To give a human example, brethren: no one annuls even a man's will, or adds to it, once it has been ratified. Now the promises were made to Abraham and to his offspring. It does not say, "And to offsprings," referring to many; but, referring to one, "And to your offspring," which is Christ. This is what I mean: the law, which came four hundred and thirty years afterward, does not annul a covenant previously ratified by God, so as to make the promise void. For if the inheritance is by the law, it is no longer by promise; but God gave it to Abraham by a promise.

Why then the law? It was added because of transgressions, till the offspring should come to whom the promise had been made; and it was ordained by angels through an intermediary. Now an intermediary implies more than one; but God is one.

Is the law then against the promises of God? Certainly not; for if a law had been given which could make alive, then righteousness would indeed be by the law. But the scripture consigned all things to sin, that what was promised to faith in Jesus Christ might be given to those who believe.

Now before faith came, we were confined under the law, kept under restraint until faith should be revealed. So that the law was our custodian until Christ came, that we might be justified by faith. But now that faith has come, we are no longer under a custodian; for in Christ Jesus you are all sons of God, through faith. For as many of you as were baptized into Christ have put on Christ. There is neither Jew nor Greek, there is neither slave nor free, there is neither male nor female; for you are all one in Christ Jesus. And if you are Christ's, then you are Abraham's offspring, heirs according to promise.

"How did it go today?" I would ask our nephew, George. It was not an idle question. George was driving a bus for a local school in order to support himself in seminary.

It was a demanding job—driving that school bus. Safety was, of course, a constant concern. So was memorizing the route, which was changed frequently as new children were added to the list to be picked up. And keeping to schedule was also a challenge with heavy traffic and tardy children.

But when I queried George on the events of the day, I usually had more in mind than safety, route, or schedule. What made the job both demanding and unpredictable were the children. Steering the bus was one thing; shepherding the children was another.

George had to keep both hands on the wheel and both eyes on the road. At the same time he had to keep the youngsters in line. Getting them to school was only part of his job. He also had to see to it that he got them there with clothes and bodies intact. Screaming, swearing, running, jumping, scratching, and pounding were all outlawed on the bus. George's difficult and thankless task was to see that the law was enforced.

Until the bus lumbered up the driveway and shuddered to a stop by the school building, George was guardian of the children—protector of their health, keeper of their morals. His answers to my questioning were both distressing and humorous—humorous because of the youngsters' unbelievable variety of antics; distressing because the children were mindless of the pain that their conduct cost George.

The school bus driver had an ancient counterpart in the Greco-Roman world of New Testament times. There were Greek slaves called guardians (literally, "child-leaders") whose responsibility was to conduct the children of the wealthy families to and from school. They were not teachers, these slaves. They were custodians assigned to guard the children on the daily journey from home to school and back again. From foolish prank, harmful mischief, and physical hurt they were to protect their wards. That assignment became the very purpose of their lives.

Paul used these guardians as a key illustration of the purpose of the law in his profound discussion of the relationship between the promise of blessing which God gave to Abraham and the law of commandments which God gave to Moses: "So that the law was our custodian until Christ came, that we might be justified by faith. But now that faith has come, we are no longer under a custodian" (Gal. 3:24–25).

These verses are the climax of a substantial argument in which Paul had been laboring to help his Galatian friends understand that God's promise to Abraham outranks the law which the Jewish teachers were trying to impose. The argument Paul pressed home may be summarized in four sentences: (1) the law does not alter the promise; (2) the law does not have the same function as the promise; (3) the law does not last as long as the promise; (4) the law does not accomplish as much as the promise.

Freedom now—our inestimable privilege as Christians—was what Paul was arguing for. To follow his arguments with mind and heart is to enhance our experience of Christian freedom.

The Law Does Not Alter the Promise

The teachers who had followed on the heels of Paul throughout Asia Minor (modern Turkey) were peddling their point of view for all they were worth. At the heart of their false teaching was the claim that the law given to Moses was an essential pillar of the Christian faith. Without circumcision, they taught, the whole house of faith would collapse. They had frightened the Galatian Christians into believing them. And Paul had to take great pains to lift this fear.

He did so by trying to show that the promise God made to Abraham has priority over the law. Paul's first argument was based on timing. The law, he reasoned, does not alter the promise, because it came after the promise by the space of over four hundred years.

He seized an illustration from legal custom and used it to seal his point: "To give a human example, brethren: no one annuls even a man's will, or adds to it, once it has been ratified. . . . This is what I mean: the law, which came four hundred and thirty years afterward, does not annul a covenant previously ratified by God, so as to make the promise void" (Gal. 3:15, 17). We catch Paul's point. When a man makes a last will or testament and has it duly witnessed, no one else has any legal right to change it or to add to it. The promise of blessing that God gave to Abraham—the promise of land to be possessed, of a nation to be fathered, of a blessing to be shared with the world—is likened to a will. It has been duly ratified by the oath of God himself. Nothing can change it. The promise is still in force, Paul announced. We can rejoice in its grace, delight in its freedom.

The mention of promise sparked two other thoughts in Paul's mind. First, the promise focuses on *Christ:* "Now the promises were made to Abraham and to his offspring. It does not say, 'And to offsprings,' referring to many; but, referring to one, 'And to your offspring,' which is Christ" (Gal. 3:16). Paul knew that what God had in mind for Abraham was not just the birth of Isaac and not just the growth of the Hebrew people. The true seed of Abraham was to be the Messiah. Matthew's Gospel sensed this when it began the New Testament with "The book of the genealogy of Jesus Christ, the son of David, the son of Abraham" (Matt. 1:1).

To put it in a word, the promise to Abraham was not just an ethnic or a national promise, given to and for Jews. It was primarily a Christian promise, because its

fulfillment came in Christ, who belongs to all people—
Jew and Gentile alike.

Paul's second thought centered in the word *inheritance*, a word which the Jewish teachers treasured
because they believed themselves to be the heirs of
Abraham, the ones to whom his spiritual legacy was
bequeathed. And in keeping with their firm convictions
about the law, they assumed that it was on those who
guard the law that the bounty of Abraham's heritage
would be bestowed. Paul refuted this conviction: "For
if the inheritance is by the law, it is no longer by
promise; but God gave it to Abraham by a promise"
(Gal. 3:18). Law and promise are two different ways
of operating. Law calls for our performance; promise
features God's pledge. Law pivots on what we do;
promise turns on what God says. The very fact that
the promise depends on God's word alone means it has
nothing to do with law. Our spiritual inheritance—the
rich blessings of God's love and grace—cannot be
earned; it can only be accepted with thanks.

The Law Does Not Have the Same Function as the Promise

Timing was the point of Paul's first argument. You
and I can enjoy our freedom from the fear of breaking
God's law, because the law came along later than the
promise and cannot alter it.

Paul's next argument had to do with the *purpose* of
the law. He anticipated the question of the Galatian
believers: if the law cannot change the promise, and
if the law is the ground of our spiritual inheritance,
why did God give it? What purpose does it serve? "It
was added because of transgressions, till the offspring

should come to whom the promise had been made . . . " (Gal. 3:19). Why the law? God gave it to show us how crooked our lives are. It is a measuring rod that tells us how far we have wandered from God's true path. It is a plumbline that calls attention to how tilted our words and deeds and motives have become. The law cannot save us, but it can help us to know how badly we need saving. A temperature chart in a hospital has no power to cure, but it serves an essential purpose in tracking the course of an illness.

Law and promise do not really war against each other; they simply have two different functions. Paul's quarrel throughout this letter was not with the law itself, but with the wrong purpose for which it had been used. The circumcision party, with their insistence that law was the key to open the Christian gate to Gentiles, were actually crowding Christ from the center of the faith. In so doing they were not only demeaning the Savior, they were also asking the law to do for men and women what it was never designed to do: ". . . for if a law had been given which could make alive, then righteousness would indeed be by the law" (Gal. 3:21).

The law was just the thermometer, not the medication. It served as a bandage to cover our sores until the great Physician could effect our healing. We were in need of more than correction. *Life* was our greatest need; we were dead in our sins, lifeless in our rebellion. The law wrote our obituary; it could not prompt our resurrection.

The Law Does Not Last as Long as the Promise

Paul carried his argument a third step. The law has to take second place in importance to the promise because it does not last as long: "Now before faith came [that is, the faith we are to have in Christ as the basis of our salvation], we were confined under the law, kept under restraint until faith should be revealed. So that the law was our custodian until Christ came, that we might be justified by faith" (Gal. 3:23–24). A key word in this argument is *until*—"until faith should be revealed," "until Christ came."

Until points to the *temporariness* of the law. When you look at the whole sweep of God's program, you see that the law came late and left early. The promise stretches from Abraham right through God's whole program to Christ's second coming, when its full blessings will be experienced. The law began with Moses, centuries after Abraham, and concluded with the crucifixion of Christ that makes our justification—our right standing with God—possible.

The purpose of the law is then fulfilled. It has shown us how sinful we are; it has kept us from being as sinful as we would have been without it; it has sharpened our guilt so that we long for justification. It has played its role. It now steps from center stage and lets the spotlight fall on Christ, who alone can bring justification and life.

Like the bus driver, it has taken us safely to school. It has kept us from destroying ourselves and others along the way. It has prepared us for the lessons of love and grace and freedom which the good news of Jesus Christ teaches.

The Law Does Not Accomplish as Much as the Promise

Paul closed his argument with a look at what the

promise achieves. Its *results* outshine those of the law. The gospel brings us into a mature relationship with God. The guardian law is no longer our authority; "for in Christ Jesus you are all sons of God, through faith" (Gal. 3:26). Not children but grownups, not slaves but sons and daughters, we live not under the constraints of law but in the freedom of the promise.

Ours is an *intimate* relationship: we were "baptized into Christ," immersed in him. He has become the setting and context of our living.

Ours is a *total* relationship: we "have put on Christ" (Gal. 3:27). We are clothed in him. His righteousness has become our garment. Like a seamless robe, he shrouds us with his gracious character. His grace—not fear of law—has become our very style of living.

Ours is a *unifying* relationship: "There is neither Jew nor Greek, there is neither slave nor free, there is neither male nor female; for you are all one in Christ Jesus" (Gal. 3:28). The false teachers had revived the terrible divisions that fractured the world of Paul's day—divisions of race, of station, of sex. The loving work of God through Christ rubs out all the lines that divide. All sons and daughters of God have equal standing—and all belong to Abraham as well (Gal. 3:29). A true Christian is Abraham's child, open to *all* the blessings of God.

Let this good news bring you freedom now. If you belong to Christ, you are an heir of the King. There is no treasure of God's grace which will be withheld from you.

7

How Can Slaves Become Sons?

Galatians 4:1-31

I mean that the heir, as long as he is a child, is no better than a slave, though he is the owner of all the estate; but he is under guardians and trustees until the date set by the father. So with us; when we were children, we were slaves to the elemental spirits of the universe. But when the time had fully come, God sent forth his Son, born of woman, born under the law, to redeem those who were under the law, so that we might receive adoption as sons. And because you are sons, God has sent the Spirit of his Son into our hearts, crying, "Abba! Father!" So through God you are no longer a slave but a son, and if a son then an heir.

Formerly, when you did not know God, you were in bondage to beings that by nature are no gods; but now that you have come to know God, or rather to be known by God, how can you turn back again to the weak and beggarly elemental spirits, whose slaves you want to be once more? You observe days, and months, and seasons, and years! I am afraid I have labored over you in vain.

Brethren, I beseech you, become as I am, for I also
have become as you are. You did me no wrong; you
know it was because of a bodily ailment that I preached
the gospel to you at first; and though my condition was
a trial to you, you did not scorn or despise me, but
received me as an angel of God, as Christ Jesus. What
has become of the satisfaction you felt? For I bear you
witness that, if possible, you would have plucked out
your eyes and given them to me. Have I then become
your enemy by telling you the truth? They make much
of you, but for no good purpose; they want to shut
you out, that you may make much of them. For a good
purpose it is always good to be made much of, and not
only when I am present with you. My little children,
with whom I am again in travail until Christ be formed
in you! I could wish to be present with you now and to
change my tone, for I am perplexed about you.

Tell me, you who desire to be under law, do you not
hear the law? For it is written that Abraham had two
sons, one by a slave and one by a free woman. But
the son of the slave was born according to the flesh, the
son of the free woman through promise. Now this is
an allegory: these women are two covenants. One is
from Mount Sinai, bearing children for slavery; she
is Hagar. Now Hagar is Mount Sinai in Arabia; she
corresponds to the present Jerusalem, for she is in
slavery with her children. But the Jerusalem above is
free, and she is our mother. For it is written,

> "Rejoice, O barren one who does not bear;
>   break forth and shout, you who are
>   not in travail;
>   for the children of the desolate one

*are many more than the children of
her that is married."*
*Now we, brethren, like Isaac, are children of promise.
But as at that time he who was born according to the
flesh persecuted him who was born according to the
Spirit, so it is now. But what does the scripture say?
"Cast out the slave and her son; for the son of the slave
shall not inherit with the son of the free woman." So,
brethren, we are not children of the slave but of the
free woman.*

Have you ever noticed the orders that parents give
to little children? Unless you yourself have been
through the ordeal of helping youngsters learn the patterns of safety and the amenities of civilization, those
commands sound incredible.

Usually they are uttered in strained and anxious
tones, sometimes edged with frenzy or disgust. I have
more in mind than the routine regimen that generations
of parents have enforced on their young: "Keep your
elbows off the table!" "Sit up straight!" "Be sure to
wash behind your ears!" "Don't leave your wagon in
the driveway!"

The orders that stun the outsider are of a more
urgent kind: "Don't stuff that bread up your nose!"
"Stop chewing your hair!" "Don't stick that hairpin
in the electric socket!" "Never let me catch you using
your good sweater to wipe your shoes!"

For children, life is a dreary series of do's and
don'ts—most of which are necessary, if only to preserve our sanity as parents. No matter how wealthy the

family, no matter how famous the parents, their children lead lives that are carefully circumscribed by rules and regulations. Obviously, some homes are more permissive than others; some households offer wider boundaries than others. But all families and all societies impose limits on what their young offspring may do or not do. Children have to be raised that way.

They sometimes chafe against those limits; they often slip beyond them to test our seriousness. All of this we understand; we did the same. We may even have viewed childhood as a form of slavery, so regulated were our movements, so ordered was our conduct.

When the Right Time Has Come

Paul drew upon this universal pattern of child-training to illustrate the difference between our pre-Christian and our Christian experience. "I mean that the heir, as long as he is a child, is no better than a slave, though he is the owner of all the estate; but he is under guardians and trustees until the date set by the father" (Gal. 4:1–2). It was a wealthy landowner that Paul used as an illustration. Though the heir of that family was marked for great wealth, destined to own the whole estate, his life was carefully regulated and managed until his father declared him to be old enough to handle the responsibilities of an adult. The English nannies who reared and trained the children of nobility would be modern examples of what Paul had in mind.

Paul made his application: "So with us; when we were children, we were slaves to the elemental spirits of the universe" (Gal. 4:3). Our pre-Christian days, Paul argued, were like a childhood; our ways and works were closely watched. We were slaves, not to the will of a wise guardian or a firm but gentle nanny, but to "elemental spirits of the universe." This difficult phrase —elemental spirits—seems to point to the religious superstitions that have kept the non-Christian world in bondage through the centuries.

Like young children in a wealthy home, the citizens of our spinning planet cannot enjoy their full inheritance as creatures of God because they are slaves to superstition. Some look to magical spells and secret ceremonies to drive away the hostile demons and to placate the good spirits. Others believe that their daily destiny is determined by the stars. Lucky numbers, private charms, personal rituals, ouiji boards, horoscopes, good luck coins—these are a few of the signs of superstition in societies both ancient and modern.

Such superstitions leave no room for freedom. They keep people edgy with uncertainty. Where do we stand with these spirits? Are they for us or against us? They sap our energy in fear. What if we do the wrong thing? What if we bungle the magic or misread the stars?

In a surprising, even shocking, way Paul seems to include *Jews* in this picture of slavery. The law, God-given, had become so abused and its purposes had become so distorted, that it became almost a form of superstition. It held its adherents in check; it bound them to its demands; it infused them with fear of its judgments.

Paul's answer to this religious superstition—the cringing fear of displeasing the deity and the heavenly spirits—was not to discount it. It was not to deny the reality of the fears or the existence of the spiritual forces that spawned them. Paul was not a secular man who limited his horizons to what could be seen and measured. He was not a materialist who scoffed at the idea of supernatural powers.

Paul's answer lay in another direction. He did not try to correct false religion by urging his hearers to become irreligious. He did not seek to spoof at their superstitions and shame them into disbelief. He gave a positive answer to the fears, the most positive answer possible: "But when the time had fully come, God sent forth his Son, born of woman, born under the law, to redeem those who were under the law, so that we might receive adoption as sons" (Gal. 4:4-5). At the right time God made possible a new relationship—that is Paul's answer. We children, under the fear of superstition, under bondage to law, can now enjoy the maturity of sonship, because our Father has declared the time to be right.

Slaves can now be sons and daughters of God because the time has "fully come." Think of all the preparation that led to the sending of God's Son. The entire Old Testament is part of that preparation. The promises to Abraham, the system of sacrifices, the hopes of a Messianic King, the prophecies of a suffering servant and a conquering Son of Man—these all have their fulfillment in that Son sent by God at the right time.

But God's preparation reached beyond the scrolls of the Old Testament and beyond his covenant with Israel. It reached to the shores of Macedonia and marched with the troops of Alexander as they planted Greek culture and language from Asia Minor to the borders of India. Thanks to Alexander's exploits, the good news of the Son was heralded through the known world in a language understood more widely than any other language had been before.

God's preparation stretched to the banks of the Tiber and ranged around Europe, the Middle East, and North Africa with the architects and engineers of Rome as they strung their arched aqueducts and surveyed their straight highways. Roman transportation, Roman peace, Roman government tied the scattered ancient strands of the world into a network of political and economic cooperation that made the traveling of the apostles and the spreading of their message easier than at any previous time.

The scattering of the Jews was also part of God's preparation. Their synagogues from Babylon to Antioch, to Alexandria, to Philippi, to Rome, became the beachheads where the Christian invasion gained a foothold on foreign shores after "the time had fully come."

Along with all of these—the Greek language, the Roman politics, the Jewish dispersion, the Old Testament prophecies—Paul had something else in mind: the proven futility of the old religion. Superstition among the pagans and legalism among the Jews had run their course. They had had centuries to try to solve the human problems of meaninglessness and guilt. But their solutions were not solutions. Millennia of subjection to the rule of spirits, centuries of clinging to the law had not produced the freedom of forgiveness or the delights of true life. Bitter, frustrated, broken, the first-century world—Jew and Gentile alike—yearned for better news.

When the New Relationship Is Formed

Then it happened: at the right time God made possible a new relationship. He broke through the gloom of paganism and legalism by sending his own Son into the midst of human life—"born of woman, born under the law" (Gal. 4:4). Total immersion in our kind of life— that is what these phrases mean. Jesus is no outsider to our circumstances. He became one of us, stirring in his mother's body and then being thrust out to live under the discipline of law like all his fellows.

The results of this divine invasion were astounding. The whole tone of our human existence was changed. A way out of our childishness and slavery was opened. A new relationship with God was formed.

Redemption and *adoption* are the two words used to describe this relationship. They are appropriate words because they belong to the language of a society where slavery was a way of life. God sent Christ "to redeem those who were under the law" (Gal. 4:5). Law— whether gentile rituals or Jewish regulations—is like a slaveowner who treats his servants like chattel, mindless of their potential and heedless of their hurts.

Redemption and adoption are legal transactions that liberate a slave and change his status. *To redeem* is to set free by the payment of a price. The price, of course, was Jesus' death.

But the new relationship does not stop with freedom; it moves on to sonship. Owners attracted to certain slaves and appreciative of their talents could legally adopt them. This often happened when the owner was childless and wanted an heir to whom to bequeath his property.

From slaves to sons and daughters—that is the biography of all who trust in Christ. At the right time, by sending his Son, God made it possible for the world to grow up, to come of age, to enter into full freedom, to enjoy the privileges of sonship.

But what is *possible* for all persons has not yet become *actual* in many lives. Occasionally we hear reports of contact with a tribe in New Guinea or the Philippines where the impact of civilization has not reached. The members of that society still live in the Stone Age, unaware of the vast improvements in hunting and agriculture that metal has brought to civilization. Sharp stones or chips of flint are their only tools and weapons. Though others have been enjoying the benefits of metallurgy for five thousand years, those tribal peoples live in ignorance of these simple technical advances.

So it is with the gospel. Christ exposed the childishness, the slavery of religious superstition two millennia ago. He thrust the whole world forward into a new age, an age of grace, of power, of freedom. Yet many persons and some peoples still live as though Christ had not been sent—yoked to law, strapped by futility, fettered in bondage.

They need to hear these words: "So through God you are no longer a slave but a son, and if a son then an heir" (Gal. 4:7). *Through God*—that phrase stands at the heart of the whole trek from slavery to sonship.

God it is who took the initiative in sending his Son. No one can redeem or adopt himself or herself. God it is who sends the Holy Spirit into our hearts, enabling us to call God "Father." So weak are we and so confused in our false religious commitments that we cannot even stammer the word *Father,* unless God the Holy Spirit makes it possible.

Through God our sonship comes. He set the right time; he formed the new relationship. Through God—Father, Son, and Spirit—freedom has become a reality. Through God, the "get your elbows off the table" and "wash behind your ears" and "don't leave your wagon in the driveway" type of religion has become the good news of grace and love.

8

Will My Faith
Cost Me My Freedom?

Galatians 5:1-15

*For freedom Christ has set us free; stand fast there-
fore, and do not submit again to a yoke of slavery.*

*Now I, Paul, say to you that if you receive circum-
cision, Christ will be of no advantage to you. I testify
again to every man who receives circumcision that he is
bound to keep the whole law. You are severed from
Christ, you who would be justified by the law; you
have fallen away from grace. For through the Spirit, by
faith, we wait for the hope of righteousness. For in
Christ Jesus neither circumcision nor uncircumcision is
of any avail, but faith working through love. You were
running well; who hindered you from obeying the
truth? This persuasion is not from him who called you.
A little leaven leavens the whole lump. I have confidence in the Lord that you will take no other view than
mine; and he who is troubling you will bear his judgment, whoever he is. But if I, brethren, still preach circumcision, why am I still persecuted? In that case the
stumbling block of the cross has been removed. I wish
those who unsettle you would mutilate themselves!*

For you were called to freedom, brethren; only do not use your freedom as an opportunity for the flesh, but through love be servants of one another. For the whole law is fulfilled in one word, "You shall love your neighbor as yourself." But if you bite and devour one another take heed that you are not consumed by one another.

The applause was deafening. The black man with the slight build relaxed and grinned as he acknowledged the cheers of the crowd. Moments before, he had been as taut as stretched leather. With his back arched like a sapling in the wind, forehead glistening like a dewy leaf in the sunlight, microphone held high like a flowering orchid, Sammy Davis, Jr., had sounded the creed of a whole generation: "I've Gotta Be Me."

The applause was deafening not only because the entertainer is popular and not only because the rendition was stirring. The applause was deafening because the audience identified with the sentiment—they felt that they had to be themselves. "I've gotta be me" is a theme song of modern freedom, a slogan of the dominant movement of our times—the drive for individual self-expression.

The mood of our times—a mood that rang through that applause—may make it hard for many to commit their lives to Jesus Christ. They sense that commitment to him may raise a conflict between their faith and their freedom, a conflict voiced in the question, "Will my faith cost me my freedom?" Or perhaps they put it another way, "Will Jesus Christ let me be me?"

Alternatives to Freedom

People who raise these questions will do well to take a look at what Paul wrote to his friends at Galatia. Freedom is not at all the natural human state, Paul had pointed out. The whole race is enslaved to superstitions, to fears of superhuman powers, to conformity to religious requirements, whether pagan or Jewish.

There could be no freedom without intervention on God's part. He had to send his Son to redeem us from slavery and to adopt us as sons; he had to send his Spirit to help us call God "Father." Far from being free, we could not even respond to God's emancipation unless he gave us the words.

Freedom was only achieved by God's initiative. And freedom can be maintained only by God's assistance. We cannot gain freedom on our own; we cannot keep freedom on our own.

Bobby Ferguson lived in the Iowa State Penitentiary. For about forty years he had lived there. In fact, he was born there. His mother was a prisoner at the time of his birth. Recently, Bobby Ferguson was released from the prison, encouraged by the warden to make a new life for himself on the outside. He could not do it. He begged the governor of Iowa and the warden of the prison to allow him to return within the guarded walls that had been his lifetime dwelling. His petition was granted, and Bobby Ferguson worked as a custodian in the penitentiary that he called home until the day he died. Freedom is hard for most of us to bear. We say we want it and then find it hard to live with. The Galatian Christians had that problem. Despite Paul's clear

preaching when he was with them and despite his firm
pleading after he had left, they were flirting again with
slavery. The alternatives to freedom are deceptive in
their attractiveness.

Legalism is one attractive alternative. It offers security, because it tells you specifically what to do. It
demands discipline and, therefore, gives you the feeling
that you are really trying hard to please God. It lends
an air of distinctiveness, as you keep regulations that
other people ignore. It promotes a sense of comradeship
among those who live by its dictates.

Despite its attractiveness, Paul warned, legalism is a
harsh, heavy yoke: "For freedom Christ has set us free;
stand fast therefore, and do not submit again to a yoke
of slavery" (Gal. 5:1).

This exhortation is sandwiched between two cogent
arguments. The first is this: trusting law for salvation
cuts us off from the inheritance promised to the heirs of
Abraham: "For it is written that Abraham had two
sons, one by a slave and one by a free woman. But the
son of the slave [Ishmael, son of Hagar] was born according to the flesh, the son of the free woman [Isaac,
son of Sarah] through promise" (Gal. 4:22–23).

Using Old Testament law, so precious to the Jewish
teachers that were putting pressure on the Galatians,
Paul argued that those who trust in law as the way to
please God may be sons of Abraham, but their mother
is Hagar the slave, not Sarah the free woman. Their
hope is not in the saving promise of God that helped
Sarah bare a child when she was past the normal age;
their hope is in fleshly efforts like Abraham's when he
tried to help God give him a son by taking a slave girl
as a substitute wife.

Paul capped this first argument with the reminder that in the Old Testament story the slave wife and her son were cast out of the family, while the son of the free woman inherited Abraham's estate and his blessing. Slavery to law leads to disinheritance by God. That was Paul's relentless conclusion.

Paul's second argument for freedom was put frankly: "Now I, Paul, say to you that if you receive circumcision, Christ will be of no advantage to you. I testify again to every man who receives circumcision that he is bound to keep the whole law. You are severed from Christ, you who would be justified by the law; you have fallen away from grace" (Gal. 5:2–4).

The troublemakers were teaching that Christ *plus* the law is the formula for salvation. Paul stepped to the blackboard and canceled that equation. God's arithmetic, Paul reasoned, is all or nothing. All law or all Christ—but no combination will do.

Paul's language was strong: "no advantage," "severed from Christ," "fallen away from grace." Either we trust Christ completely or we are not trusting him at all. Either we cast ourselves on his grace or we spurn that grace. No one can cross a bridge while keeping one foot on the bank. A life raft does no good for the person who still clings to the sinking ship.

Legalism will not do. What appears to be an appealing alternative to true freedom loses its attraction when we see what it does to those who try to please God that way.

License is the other alternative that Paul considers: "For you were called to freedom, brethren; only do not use your freedom as an opportunity for the flesh, but through love be servants of one another. For the whole law is fulfilled in one word, 'You shall love your neighbor as yourself.' But if you bite and devour one another take heed that you are not consumed by one another" (Gal. 5:13–15).

Overreaction is not the answer to any problem, especially legalism. If legalism says, "You must do it this way if God is to be pleased," license says, "I'll do it my own way and let God make the best of it." These violent swings of the pendulum often happen, but no balance is to be found at the extremes.

The flesh is as ruthless a master as the law. Jealousy, hatred, lust, strife exact their dues. Legalism is a menace to the human spirit, but so is lawlessness.

To have no limits, to cast off restraint, to shun convention, to walk on the wild side may look attractive at first. But the wounds that come from abandonment to rebellion pain their bearers at least as much as the hurts inflicted by the lash of the law.

Aspects of Freedom

Not lawlessness but love is the fruit of freedom. To men and women being courted by law Paul said, "Let this be the law to whose wooing you give in—the law of *love*." "For in Christ Jesus neither circumcision nor uncircumcision is of any avail, but faith working through love" (Gal. 5:6).

Freedom is freedom for love, freedom for treating others with the concern and dignity with which God has treated us. Neither law nor license knows this aspect of freedom.

Law leads to pride or despair. The person who thinks he is pleasing God through law may have a smug self-righteousness that holds his head so high he cannot even see the needs of others. And the person who fails to please God by breaking the law is so consumed by his own problems that he has no energy to reach out to other persons. Besides, he is sure they would not want his love anyway, so wretched is his view of himself.

License leads to boredom and frustration. The woman who seeks pleasure doing what she wants to do is caught in a dilemma: if she finds the pleasure she seeks, she will wallow in boredom; if she does not find it, she will stew in frustration. And neither boredom nor frustration is good soil for love to flourish in.

Freedom is freedom for *hope*, the hope that all of God's righteous plans will come to pass, that God's good kingdom will establish its rule among the human family: "For through the Spirit, by faith, we wait for the hope of righteousness" (Gal. 5:5).

Neither the legalist nor the libertine can wait with this kind of hope. The legalist lives on edge, fearful that he may break the law and incur God's wrath. The libertine lives for the present, mindless of the future implications of his conduct.

But the free person waits for the hope that all will be right, that all the promises of God will come true, that God's whole will is to be done. This is freedom from uncertainty; the outcome of our faith is as sure as the death and resurrection of Christ on which it is grounded. This is freedom from fear; God's own Spirit dwells within us as a guarantee that hope will not miscarry.

Will my faith cost me my freedom? No, but absence of faith will. Will my faith cost me my freedom? No, but ultimate trust in anything or anyone but Christ will. Will my faith cost me my freedom? No, it will set me free to love and hope, to discover meaning *now* and certainty *then*.

Perhaps the best answer one can give to the question is this: Your faith will not cost you your freedom, because Christ himself is free. Paul was continually suspicious of the motives of the false teachers: "They make much of you, but for no good purpose; they want to shut you out [i.e., block you off from fellowship with me], that you may make much of them" (Gal. 4:17).

About Jesus' motives Paul had no question at all. Jesus was a free man, the one ". . . who loved me and gave himself for me" (Gal. 2:20). Bossy, pushy people —dictatorial types—have to have everything under control. They lead by taking away freedom. The Good Shepherd leads by offering true freedom to all who follow.

Will my faith cost me my freedom? No, it will give the only freedom possible, the freedom that comes from knowing that all is well between us and God, because Jesus Christ has made it well.

If the audience in a television studio could burst into applause at a song of false freedom, what should be the response of us to whom *true* freedom has so freely been granted? Let's hear it for Jesus Christ!

9

How Much Can Christ Change My Life?

Galatians 5:16-24

But I say, walk by the Spirit, and do not gratify the desires of the flesh. For the desires of the flesh are against the Spirit, and the desires of the Spirit are against the flesh; for these are opposed to each other, to prevent you from doing what you would. But if you are led by the Spirit you are not under the law. Now the works of the flesh are plain: fornication, impurity, licentiousness, idolatry, sorcery, enmity, strife, jealousy, anger, selfishness, dissension, party spirit, envy, drunkenness, carousing, and the like. I warn you, as I warned you before, that those who do such things shall not inherit the kingdom of God. But the fruit of the Spirit is love, joy, peace, patience, kindness, goodness, faithfulness, gentleness, self-control; against such there is no law. And those who belong to Christ Jesus have crucified the flesh with its passions and desires.

Freedom is much more easily lost than kept. A distinguished Russian novelist has recently made this point. In his account of the Soviet system of labor camps called *Gulag Archipelago*, Alexander Solzhenitsyn puzzled over the fact that the freedom gained in the Russian revolution of 1917 was so quickly surrendered to a new totalitarian regime: "We lacked enough love of freedom. And even more a consciousness of the real situation. We spent ourselves in one unrestrained outburst in 1917, and then we made haste to be submissive. We submitted with pleasure" (*Sydney Morning Herald*, January 8, 1974).

"We lacked enough love of freedom. . . . We submitted with pleasure." These sentences could serve as a brief biography for the whole human family. Left to ourselves we will give our freedom away almost every time. Paul had read this human tendency with accuracy, and urged his friends in Galatia to stiffen against it: "For freedom Christ has set us free; stand fast therefore, and do not submit again to a yoke of slavery. . . . For you were called to freedom, brethren; only do not use your freedom as an opportunity for the flesh, but through love be servants of one another" (Gal. 5:1, 13).

What are the forces that put our freedom in constant jeopardy? Paul has already named a couple—and not only named them, but described them in some detail. *Religious superstition* is one: "So with us; when we were children, we were slaves to the elemental spirits of the universe. . . . but now that you have come to know God, or rather to be known by God, how can you turn back again to the weak and beggarly elemental spirits, whose slaves you want to be once more? You observe days, and months, and seasons, and years!" (Gal. 4:3, 9–10).

Legalism is another force that threatens our freedom: "For all who rely on works of the law are under a curse; for it is written, 'Cursed be every one who does not abide by all things written in the book of the law, and do them.' . . . Now before faith came, we were confined under the law, kept under restraint until faith should be revealed. . . . I testify again to every man who receives circumcision that he is bound to keep the whole law" (Gal. 3:10, 23; 5:3). *Cursed, confined, bound*—these are Paul's strong terms to picture the enslaving effect of legalism. Paul did not hesitate to teach that Jews who trust in circumcision for salvation are slaves, not free people. His interpretation of the story of Sarah and Hagar made that plain: "Now this is an allegory: these women are two covenants. One is from Mount Sinai, bearing children for slavery; she is Hagar. Now Hagar is Mount Sinai in Arabia; she corresponds to the present Jerusalem, for she is in slavery with her children" (Gal. 4:24–25). Like Abraham's slave wife Hagar, the present Jerusalem (that is, the Jewish religious system) would not free itself and could not offer freedom to its offspring.

The Works Our Flesh Produces

"We lacked enough love of freedom. . . . We submitted with pleasure." The Russian problem is, in fact, the human problem. And, as in the case of Russia in 1917, the threats to freedom do not come from outside alone. We also carry them within ourselves. Religious superstition and legalism are not our only potential slavemasters. Our own human drives and desires also can lash us to the oars like galley slaves, or chain our legs like laborers in a prison camp.

For the Russians, freedom from Czarist oppression
soon became submission to Stalinist dictates. For Christians, it can be the same. Though we have been redeemed by the work of Christ, and though we have
been adopted as sons and daughters of God, we are still
vulnerable to slavery—slavery to the *flesh.*

"But I say, walk by the Spirit, and do not gratify the
desires of the flesh. For the desires of the flesh are
against the Spirit, and the desires of the Spirit are against
the flesh; for these are opposed to each other, to prevent
you from doing what you would" (Gal. 5:16–17).
Conflict is a part of Christian living. Because Christian
living is human living, it is subject to our human desires
and appetites. At the same time, it is a new life in the
Spirit. The old and the new clash, and this clashing
drains our energies and distracts our attention so that we
are often diverted from doing the will of God.

Paul gave no simple solution to this conflict. The
Spirit of God stands in opposition to our fleshly urges
as well as to our legalistic tendencies. Neither bondage
to law nor abandonment to flesh—neither legalism nor
libertinism—is a spiritual state: "But if you are led by
the Spirit you are not under the law" (Gal. 5:18). Paul
inserted this reminder that neither extreme—careful
regulation nor carefree rebellion—is really the work of
the Spirit. The Spirit will make a crucial difference in
our lives, but only if we really know how drastically we
need his help, how radically our lives need to change.

Paul used a forceful means to show us this. Mercilessly
he spelled out one by one the terrible works that human
flesh can produce.

He began with *sexual sins:* immorality, impurity,
licentiousness. Certainly in the ancient world—and

probably in the modern—these sexual sins were the most obvious examples of the works of the flesh. Prostitution was not only legal in Paul's day, it was part of the religious system. *Immorality* was practiced in the pagan shrines as part of the ritual which was thought to keep order and prosperity in the universe. From emperor to slave, immorality was standard practice.

Impurity reminds us that indecency is defiling. The human spirit and body were made for better things than moral looseness. The immoral person not only breaks God's law, he contaminates himself and degrades those he uses.

Licentiousness carries with it a note of recklessness. It speaks of willful, flagrant, open violation of God's call to chastity. It parades its wickedness in shameless fashion. Degradation has come to a sorry stage when it no longer is embarrassed to be known.

No wonder the Spirit of God wars against this kind of conduct. He knows the true purposes of our sexuality. He knows that God made us male and female for purposes of communion and caring and parenthood. The desires of the Spirit are against fleshly lusts, because the Spirit knows what we can be and how much Christ wants to change us.

Paul's next category of works of the flesh describes our *religious sins:* idolatry, sorcery—incorrect worship of God and illicit use of divine power. The ancients were steeped in both. God was demeaned, and people were enslaved by these false systems of religion. Idolatry led to sorcery. Having missed the true knowledge of God, mankind had no choice but to try to control its fate by magic, including the use of drugs—which was part of the practice of sorcery. Evil powers were fear-

some and had to be warded off one's friends and family
and unleashed against one's foes.

No wonder the Spirit of God does battle with the
desires of the flesh. His true knowledge and his full
power stand in endless opposition to idolatry and sorcery, which debase our worship and damage our personal relationships. The changes that God's Spirit longs
to bring are always for the better.

Paul's longest list of fleshly works has to do with
social sins: enmity, strife, jealousy, anger, selfishness,
dissension, party spirit, envy. Human history is a docu-
mentary film in which these disturbing tendencies are
featured. Divisions of race, nation, class, station, sex
have carved our human family into a legion of fearful,
defensive, bigoted, hostile groupings.

Left on our own, we find splitting much easier than
merging. We divide for our protection and then spend
endless energies in protecting these divisions.

No wonder the Spirit of God is ever challenging our
factiousness and trying to build us into true community
within the church. The body of Christ is one—no Jew,
no Gentile, no slave, no free, no male, no female. All
the barriers we build God's Spirit desires to break down
as he shows us how much Christ can change our lives.

Paul concluded this seamy list with some *personal
sins:* drunkenness, carousing, and the like. Here life has
hit bottom. Escape is seen as the only solution. Whether
from guilt, boredom, fear, or meaninglessness, people
run for the relief of alcohol. Problems and failures can
barely be seen in the twilight of stupor induced by
drinking.

No wonder the Spirit, whose name is *Holy*, desires
otherwise for us. The real world of God's powerful

grace is much to be preferred to the fantasies of intoxication. "And do not get drunk with wine, for that is debauchery; but be filled with the Spirit" (Eph. 5:18) was the advice that Paul gave other Christians when he was encouraging them to let Christ change their lives.

The Fruit God's Spirit Grows

"We lacked enough love of freedom. . . . We submitted with pleasure." That Russian tragedy need not be the last word. Freedom is possible. The Holy Spirit, whose desires run counter to the works of our flesh, can make it so.

The contest for freedom which wages within us is not at a stalemate. The Spirit has ways of winning. And his victories do us good. His desires for us are desires for our best.

Even a cursory glance at the fruit God's Spirit grows will confirm that. The Spirit changes our lives by helping us *to respond to God's good news* in love, joy, and peace.

The commitment that God made to us when he affirmed our dignity and demonstrated his concern by sending his Son, we make to others. *Love* this is called. It is part of God's good news which we receive with gratitude and share with enthusiasm.

Because God's commitment to us is unreserved, unconditional, joy and peace result from it. Joy, because nothing can alter or undo this good news. We are loved and accepted. Peace, because all basic problems of relationship have been settled. Our warfare with God is at an end. Our struggles with each other can now find settlement.

The Spirit changes our lives by helping us *to appro-*

priate Christ's character in patience, kindness, and goodness. These are all characteristics of God, who is
longsuffering toward our waywardness, kindhearted toward our sinfulness, and generous toward our poverty.

And the Spirit changes our lives by helping us *to
imitate Christ's conduct* in faithfulness, gentleness, and
self-control. Reliable even under the most trying circumstances, restrained in his use of power when that
power could have done harm, and controlled in his
emotions and passions, Jesus pioneered a whole new
way of life, a way of life that needed no laws to regulate it because it was governed by God's best law of
love.

His Spirit will do the same for us. "And those who
belong to Christ Jesus have crucified the flesh with its
passions and desires" (Gal. 5:24). The cross won the
victory, the victory beyond our winning. Without that
crucifixion the flesh would have won the whole war.

But now it is doomed. The battle has been won. Our
task is to sign the armistice and get on with the pursuits
of peace. Let there be among us no lack of love of freedom. Let us submit with pleasure not to the slaveries of
human desire but to the freedom of the Spirit's guidance. As we do, we will live in ever-growing wonder
at how much Christ has changed our lives.

10

How Practical
Is Christian Love?

Galatians 5:25-6:10

*If we live by the Spirit, let us also walk by the Spirit.
Let us have no self-conceit, no provoking of one another, no envy of one another.*

*Brethren, if a man is overtaken in any trespass, you
who are spiritual should restore him in a spirit of gentleness. Look to yourself, lest you too be tempted. Bear
one another's burdens, and so fulfil the law of Christ.
For if any one thinks he is something, when he is nothing, he deceives himself. But let each one test his own
work, and then his reason to boast will be in himself
alone and not in his neighbor. For each man will have to
bear his own load.*

*Let him who is taught the word share all good things
with him who teaches.*

*Do not be deceived; God is not mocked, for what-
ever a man sows, that he will also reap. For he who sows
to his own flesh will from the flesh reap corruption; but
he who sows to the Spirit will from the Spirit reap
eternal life. And let us not grow weary in well-doing,*

for in due season we shall reap, if we do not lose heart.
So then, as we have opportunity, let us do good to all
men, and especially to those who are of the household of
faith.

I suppose every way of life has its acid tests, its ways
of separating good metal from cheap, outstanding performance from ordinary. The housewife who can feed
three extra guests without warning, the pilot who can
land a two engine plane with only one engine working,
the quarterback who can make the first down when it is
third and thirteen, the batter who can usually move his
man from first to third, the basketball player who can
make both the field goal and the free throw when his
team needs three points, the pastor who can minister
gracefully to a family racked by a suicide—these have
all passed the acid test.

Knowing how to put theory into practice is part of
what is required. We have all read books on such sub-
jects. We *know* in our minds how to cope with extraordinary situations. But to *do* this coping is something
else.

Anxiety sets in, if not panic. And we find ourselves
fumbling in situations when we thought we were well
rehearsed.

The expert has been trained to deal with this by over-
learning. The pilot practices emergency procedures until he can follow them blindfolded. The golfer spends
hours in the rough, behind trees, and in the sand traps.
The cook tries the recipe for souffle a number of times
before she risks it with company. In each case, possible

problems are anticipated, corrective procedures are practiced, and each step is rehearsed in a way that makes it virtually routine.

Yet with all this preparation, the unexpected may still occur, and the truly proficient person will have to demonstrate his or her skill by improvising on the spot. My brother John once broke a viola string in the midst of a musical competition. He adjusted his fingering patterns and completed the solo on the other three strings.

Acid tests these are, which tell how good we are at our profession. The Christian life also has some acid tests. Can we really put into action what we believe about love? Can we make Christian love as practical as it was meant to be? This was the acid test with which Paul closed his letter to the Galatians.

Christian freedom is freedom to love in the power of the Holy Spirit. Neither legalism nor license offers this kind of freedom. Both are occupied with performance. Both are consumed with self-interest. Love is the last thing that the rebel or the conformist has in mind. At least not *Christian* love.

But for Paul, love is the acid test that shows the true gold of our discipleship from the fool's gold of other walks of life. "Faith working through love" is what really counts with God. (Gal. 5:6); *love* is the word that fulfills the whole law (Gal. 5:14). Love tops the menu among the fruit of God's Spirit and gives flavor to all the rest (Gal. 5:22).

Love Regulates Competition

In these brief comments on love, Paul had time only to mention its importance. Then he went on to describe

its function: "If we live by the Spirit, let us also walk
by the Spirit. Let us have no self-conceit, no provoking
of one another, no envy of one another" (Gal. 5:25–
26).

How practical is Christian love? It is so practical that
it recognizes its permanent dependence on the Holy
Spirit. "If we live by the Spirit"—here Paul reached
back to what he had said in earlier discussions: ". . .
Having begun with the Spirit, are you now ending with
the flesh?" (Gal. 3:3). No Christian life begins until
the Spirit sparks our faith and helps us call God
"Father" (Gal. 4:6). No Christian life can move forward to maturity—that is what Paul meant by "walk by
the Spirit"—without the Spirit's guidance and support.

A specific problem where the Spirit's help is essential
has to do with competition among Christians. One
might argue that competition is a special hurdle for believers to get over because we care so deeply about what
we believe and how we live. Here is a case where our
virtues beget our vices. Doctrine is important. After
all, it is God's truth. We are obligated to believe it with
a passion. Such passionate belief makes it easy to look
down on those who interpret the faith differently and
to puff ourselves up in the knowledge that we are right.
Paul warned another church against that inflating self-
conceit: " . . . 'Knowledge' puffs up, but love builds
up. If anyone imagines that he knows something, he
does not yet know as he ought to know. But if one
loves God, one is known by him" (1 Cor. 8:1–3).

Let your love regulate your drive to competition.
To build up your own ego at someone else's expense, to

provoke a fellow Christian to debate or conflict, to envy the possessions or accomplishments of another is to question the love of God. It is to treat someone else differently from the way God has treated us; it is to say that God's love for me is not enough, because I also want what you have.

Love Restores the Fallen

Granted that self-conceit, provocation, and envy are attitudes that the Spirit wants to sweep out of his church, there still remains the task of dealing with brothers or sisters who fall into open sin. Their situation cannot be ignored. But how is it—or rather, how are they—to be handled. With his usual realism Paul confronted the question directly: "Brethren, if a man is overtaken in any trespass, you who are spiritual should restore him in a spirit of gentleness. Look to yourself, lest you too be tempted" (Gal. 6:1).

How practical is Christian love? It is so practical that it makes restoration, not criticism, its prime ambition. It seeks to restore the fallen.

Paul's tender tone was itself an example to his hearers. "Brethren" he called them. His earlier language had been stronger: "I am astonished that you are so quickly deserting him who called you. . . . O foolish Galatians! Who has bewitched you? . . . Are you so foolish?" (Gal. 1:6; 3:1, 3). Now his own mission was restoration. He was confident that the Spirit's work among them would thrive. He himself demonstrated the fruit of the Spirit in his own life by calling them "Brethren." Whatever confusion they had endured, whatever misunderstandings they were snared in, whatever temptations they had nearly succumbed to, they were his brethren, bought by Christ, born of the Spirit.

Restoring the fallen is a *spiritual* task. Paul dipped his pen in the ink with which he had written of the Spirit's ministry. "You who are spiritual should restore him." A fleshly reaction would be to gloat in the person's failure or to envy his license to sin. The spiritual reaction is not to condemn or to imitate but to restore.

Restoring the fallen is a *gentle* task. It is an ideal place to test that gentleness or meekness which is among the Spirit's finest fruit. Think how vulnerable a man or woman is when overtaken in trespass, caught up in a flagrant sin open to the eyes of all the church. What an opportunity for self-righteousness to display itself! What a circumstance for the powerful to stomp on the fallen. That is just what meekness will not do. It uses power gently. It keeps its emotions in check. It uses its quiet strength for the healing of the hurts. Meekness is a practical expression of Christian love.

Restoring the fallen is a *humbling* task. A brother overtaken in a trespass is a lesson to the whole church. The plight of one could be the plight of all. No room for pride beside the body of a fallen brother. Only room for watchfulness. No time for prayers of presumption thanking God that it could not happen to us. Only time for humility, pleading with God not to lead us into temptation but to deliver us from the evil one. Humility is a practical expression of Christian love.

Spiritually, gently, humbly, love does its work. None of this will succeed, however, unless the person who has slipped in his Christian walk really wants to be helped. If the person remains impenitent, discipline —not restoration—is the only route possible. Yet even discipline must be done in love. Every effort toward finding out the true facts must be made; every possibility of restoration must be pursued. If the person is finally removed from leadership in the church or even banned from membership, it must be with the persistent hope that repentance will take place so that restoration may follow.

Love Shares the Burden

Love is more than an emergency operation. It not only seeks to deal with the extraordinary events in the church like the tragedy of a lapse into sin, but it also seeks to give steady day by day help to those whose burdens are beyond their managing: "Bear one another's burdens, and so fulfil the law of Christ" (Gal. 6:2).

This caring for others—not religious regulations like circumcision—is the true law of life, the law that Christ followed, the law that Christ commanded: "For the Son of man also came not to be served but to serve, and to give his life as a ransom for many" (Mark 10:45). "A new commandment I give to you, that you love one another; even as I have loved you, that you also love one another" (John 13:34).

Love puts rather precise demands on those who seek to live on its terms. First, it reminds us that *no one is too good to need help or to give help.* The faith is a brotherhood, which implies an equality of standing before the Father. All that we use to help others is a gift of grace. All that we need to shoulder our loads in life can only be supplied by grace. Grace is the great leveler that knocks down pride and self-righteousness. It makes us concerned enough to offer help and humble enough to ask for help: "For if anyone thinks he is something, when he is nothing, he deceives himself" (Gal. 6:3).

The second demand of love is this: *it teaches us to carry all of our own load that we can.* Love sets us free from rash comparisons or harsh competition. It releases us from the temptation to increase our dignity at someone else's expense. It reminds us that, though we may sometimes have burdens we need help with, most of the time, like good soldiers we can carry our own pack and still have a bit of energy left over to help a fellow trooper: "For each man will have to bear his own load" (Gal. 6:5).

Love Rewards the Teacher

For Paul, Christian love is so practical that it tugs at our purse strings: "Let him who is taught the word share all good things with him who teaches" (Gal. 6:6). *Love helps us sort out our priorities.* It focuses our attention on the great acts of God in Scripture, acts that made our salvation possible. And love connects the spiritual and the material in an uncuttable way. As God gave his Son because of his love, as God gave us his goods because of his love, so we give in return. There is no gap between our discipleship and our stewardship. The one leads to the other.

Our love for God drives us to hear his word. But it also drives us to share our goods with him or her who teaches.

How practical is Christian love? It is tough enough to deal with difficult problems and tender enough to feel deep hurts. It resembles Christ's own lofty life and reaches to the mundane resources of our bank accounts. It is practical, yet spiritual. It is practical because it is spiritual. It is the work of God's Spirit leading us to be experts in what counts most—to pass the acid tests in the art of living.

II

What Really Counts with God?

Galatians 6:11-18

See with what large letters I am writing to you with my own hand. It is those who want to make a good showing in the flesh that would compel you to be circumcised, and only in order that they may not be persecuted for the cross of Christ. For even those who receive circumcision do not themselves keep the law, but they desire to have you circumcised that they may glory in your flesh. But far be it from me to glory except in the cross of our Lord Jesus Christ, by which the world has been crucified to me, and I to the world. For neither circumcision counts for anything, nor uncircumcision, but a new creation. Peace and mercy be upon all who walk by this rule, upon the Israel of God.

Henceforth let no man trouble me; for I bear on my body the marks of Jesus.

The grace of our Lord Jesus Christ be with your spirit, brethren. Amen.

The Bangkok boatman momentarily took his hands

off the helm, held them together palm to palm, and raised them to his face in a gesture of worship. We were passing one of the shrines of Buddha along the Chao Phraya River, and the boatman did not dare ignore the image of his god.

The workman beside the ruins of ancient Baalbek stretched his tiny mat out on the ground, knelt in the direction of Mecca, and began to pray. The muezzin in the tower had chanted his call to prayer, and this Lebanese workman, like all good Muslims, had responded, despite the string of American tourists that stared as they filed by him.

The farmer reverently approached the shrine beside the village pool in the Indian state of Andhra Pradesh and poured a glass of water over the image of the god Mahadev. The burning sun of a tropical summer was beating down on the idol and Hindu custom called for this act of devotion to keep the god cool.

The truck driver climbed into the cab at the truck stop just west of Omaha and gently rubbed the rabbit's foot on his key chain. He had to roll for sixteen hours along the expressway and needed all the luck he could get.

To be on the good side of a god or the gods—that is what all these gestures have in common. Symptoms they are, these acts of ritual or magic, of our deep human commitment to powers and forces beyond us. No one who believes in supernatural realities—and there seem to be very few true atheists—wants to risk the displeasure of whatever it is that he or she worships.

What really counts with God? is a question asked and answered in virtually every culture. The Bangkok boatman bowed to Buddha; the Baalbek workman prayed to Allah; the Indian farmer eased the discomfort of Mahadev; the Omaha trucker rubbed the good luck charm. Each in his own way wanted to do what counts with his god.

It was to this basic question that Paul returned in his letter to the struggling Christians at Galatia. The issue was so important that he seized the pen from the scribe who had been taking dictation and wrote the last words with his own distinct handwriting: "See with what large letters I am writing to you with my own hand" (Gal. 6:11).

Paul was personally committed *to set the matter straight.* He knew that to make an error here was to miss the whole meaning of life. To give the wrong answer to the question of what counts with God was to send his friends on a flight to futility.

For this they needed no encouragement from him. The false teachers were personally committed *to lead their lives astray:* "It is those who want to make a good showing in the flesh that would compel you to be circumcised, and only in order that they may not be persecuted for the cross of Christ. For even those who receive circumcision do not themselves keep the law, but they desire to have you circumcised that they may glory in your flesh" (Gal. 6:12–13). Three vital mistakes these teachers of the circumcision were making. First, they compromised their beliefs to avoid persecution. Second, they taught that it was possible for human beings to keep the law and, therefore, please God. They underestimated the power of sin in their own lives and the lives of their followers. Third, they put more emphasis on their own success in gaining converts than they did on the spiritual welfare of those converts.

because] legal protection afforded Judai a way to avoid stops

Their boast, their glory, their pride, was in the badge of circumcision, not the work of God. They failed the fundamental test—they did not know what really counts with God.

Our Rejoicing in the Cross

Paul made a night and day type of contrast between himself and the Jewish Christians who were trying to lock up the Galatians to law. ". . . they [the Jewish Christians] . . . glory in your flesh" (Gal. 6:13). The center of their attention, the source of their satisfaction, was in human achievement. They gloated over the converts they had made. Their measure of success was the number of men they circumcised.

It is something entirely different that causes Paul to boast: "But far be it from me to glory except in the cross of our Lord Jesus Christ, by which the world has been crucified to me, and I to the world" (Gal. 6:14).

Paul rejoiced in the cross *because of whose work it is*. Circumcision is a *human* operation performed by one man on another. The crucifixion is a *divine* transaction in which the Father in heaven sent his Son to earth to accomplish our salvation. It is God's work—the cross of Christ—backed by his love; we can, we should, rejoice in it.

And Paul rejoiced in the cross *because of the work it does*. The cross was the site of Jesus' death. But he did not die alone. The *world* was crucified with him. This was Paul's vivid way of saying that nothing else counts with God for our salvation but what Jesus did. The world is as good as dead in God's sight. "The world has been crucified to me"—its temptations to self-sufficiency, its fearful religious systems, its immoral and

fleshly values no longer count. The cross has cancelled
them, rendered them null and void.

"And I [have been crucified] to the world"—Paul's
own appetites and desires had been changed: no longer
did he trust his own works to bring him favor in God's
eyes; no longer did he measure his success by man's
approval; no longer did he boast of his ethnic heritage
and his religious background.

Freedom now was his experience, an experience in
which all of God's people were to share. The cross had
won a victory worthy of continual celebration. Up till
Christ's crucifixion, the world seemed to be the winner.
Its values were in vogue; its religions were practiced;
its temptations were yielded to.

Now Christ had made the ultimate difference. By his
death he had put to death the former champion. The
great dictator that held human minds in darkness and
human bodies in subjection had been toppled. No wonder Paul's attention was pinned to the cross; no wonder
his rejoicing rang with exuberance: "But far be it from
me to glory except in the cross of our Lord Jesus
Christ. . . . "

What really counts with God? That we rejoice in
the cross. Paul knew that this glorying in the death of
Christ was not out of place. He knew what God himself
thought of the cross: his love had prompted it; his will
had insisted on it; his Son had offered himself on it. Of
course, God wants us to rejoice in the cross. When we
do, our joy and God's joy meet.

Our Renewal through the Cross

God had more in mind than our gladness when he
commissioned his Son to die. He longed for our restora-

tion. It was this that Paul highlighted next: "For neither circumcision counts for anything, nor uncircumcision, but a new creation" (Gal. 6:15).

The last word from the cross was not death. True, Christ died there and with him died the world's domination and our subjection to it. But the cross' final word was one of life. "A new creation" is possible because of what Jesus did. What really counts with God is not just our rejoicing in the cross but our *renewal* through the cross.

The boatman in Bangkok, the workman at Baalbek, the farmer in Andhra Pradesh, the truck driver in midwestern America are all symbols of the old creation. They illustrate the ways of the world which Christ put to death and seeks to create anew. Their religious practices and superstitions do not count with God because they all bypass the cross. They are human longings, human efforts, human drives which cannot please God. Something new is needed. Something so new, so different, so radical that it is called a *new creation*.

More religion is not what God wants. Circumcision and the law that went with it offered plenty of that. But salvation did not come that way. Nor was irreligion the answer. No merit was to be found in rejecting circumcision and seeking to live like a pagan Gentile.

Change is needed—sharp, lasting, drastic change. We cannot bring that change ourselves. It is beyond our reach. All our human attempts to change only serve to deepen our predicament. If it is wrong for us to try to save ourselves, it is doubly wrong for us to redouble our efforts to save ourselves.

Creation is the word Paul chose to describe the

change. It is the right word because it fixes our eyes on
God. Who else can create? Who else can bring life
from death, light from darkness, day from night?

A new creation is what counts, according to Paul.
What counts with God, in other words, is what he himself does. That makes sense. What can we offer him
that he does not already have? What can we tell him
that he does not already know?

What counts with God is our renewal through the
cross. *This renewal brings dramatic, personal change.*
Freedom is the best single word we can find to describe
this change. It is freedom from bondage to law, freedom
from fear of demons, freedom from pangs of guilt,
freedom from slavery to flesh. It is freedom to do the
right things for the right reasons, freedom to approach
God as Father, freedom to let the Spirit grow his fruit
within us.

This renewal links us to God's total program. A new
creation is God's central purpose. He is in the process
of making all things new. Sin and death are being dealt
with. Creation itself will be transformed when the new
heavens and the new earth appear. Persons who meet
Christ at the cross, who draw on the grace of forgiveness, who surrender their own hopes for salvation and
accept God's gift are part of this new program. They—
we—become actors in the greatest drama of history—
the drama in which God is working out his will on
earth as effectively as it is done in heaven.

The final results of the new creation are yet to be
seen. But from the beauty and density of the blossoms,
we can judge what the fruit will be like.

Paul gave us a hint in his closing words: "Peace and

mercy be upon all who walk by this rule, upon the Israel of God" (Gal. 6:16). These words pulsate with comfort and security. They sing out the good news that God is for us, and all is well. To glory in the cross, to take part in the new creation, is to walk by the rule that God has laid down, the rule that we are to depend only on him for life and salvation.

Even suffering can be put in perspective when we know what counts with God: "Henceforth let no man trouble me; for I bear on my body the marks of Jesus" (Gal. 6:17). These words testify to the *patience and confidence* that Paul had as part of the new creation. No one could intimidate him by threat of persecution. He had already endured plenty of it, and he viewed it as part of his fellowship with Jesus. Any cross that Paul carried he viewed as a partnership with Christ, who had carried the cross for him. Far from separating us from Christ, suffering should unite us with him. To suffer is to share in common with Christ the deepest experience of life. Paul proudly displayed his scars as marks of his participation in the ministry of the Savior. Like battle ribbons they marked him as a hero of the faith.

For his last word in the letter, Paul returned to what was his first word—*grace:* "The grace of our Lord Jesus Christ be with your spirit, brethren. Amen" (Gal. 6:18). The new creation is bathed in grace. It can live no other way. We who are Abraham's sons and daughters by faith, we who are the Israel of God, God's new people, are totally dependent on grace. And because we are, we can call each other "brethren." We belong to each other through the ties of the cross, through the freedom of forgiveness, through the assurance of the Spirit.

We are brethren because, together, we have abandoned a false trust in religious gestures, in human works, in magic rituals, in good luck charms. We are brethren together because we know what really counts with God.

And we know one thing more. We know that what really counts with God is what really counts!

CONCLUSION

We have moved quickly through one of the master-pieces in the annals of literature. We need feel no guilt. Our study should not be likened to the frenzied tour group that tries to see the Louvre in Paris or the British Museum in an hour.

We shall have lots of opportunities to come back. Galatians has been with us a long time. It is not in danger of disappearing.

Hurrying through it is not a bad idea. Think of the speed with which the first hearers must have heard its words. Undoubtedly whoever read it to them took them through it at one sitting—or standing. Only later did they have the leisure to analyze its paragraphs and sense the detailed strength of its arguments.

On first hearing, what they found was that it rang with good news. It reminded them that the gospel of freedom which Paul had first preached to them was backed by his authority as a true apostle and by the testimony of God's Spirit. It told them that Christ had done new things for them by his death and resurrection. It assured them that they belonged to a long line of people who found new life by committing themselves to God—a line that stretched back to Abraham.

Above all it told them that Jesus has set them free from bondage to legal regulations and religious rituals. Freedom, not circumcision, was to be their new watchword—a freedom that was neither license nor rebellion, an open freedom without angry rhetoric or menacing gestures, a loving freedom that took them as they were, a powerful freedom that could make them what they wanted to be.

All this they heard that first time round. And centuries of study by the best minds and hearts of the Christian Church have only supported those first impressions.

If we have heard what they heard, then God's Spirit has done his work. He who first stirred the mind and tongue of a concerned apostle has again made his Word irresistible. Where that has happened we have gotten a fresh grasp of freedom. Or better yet, Christ's fresh freedom has more firmly grasped us.

He's 'kid-napping' – in a sleeping kid